More Than Sales

Seeking God's Heart
For Your
Direct Sales Business

K.E. Sipps

NABI Press

Library of Congress Cataloging-in-Publication Data is on file at the
Library of Congress in Washington, DC.
ISBN-10: 0615960766
ISBN-13: 978-0615960760 (NABI Press)

DEDICATION

To my Lord and Savior.
Yes Lord, I would still write it if you were my only reader.

CONTENTS

A Note from Karen

Dear Friend,

More Than Sales was born at a direct sales leadership retreat, although I didn't realize it at the time. I'd been asked to provide the devotional for each of the four days we were at the retreat. I could have scoured the internet to find something suitable for our theme (Mission: Possible) but I felt strongly led to write them myself. If you'd like to read them, you can find them at the very end of this book. Those first four sparked a flame to truly seek out what God's heart is for those of us in Direct Sales and I cannot wait to share His heart with YOU.

Let's be clear, though. Of all the things this book is, there are two things it is NOT.

It's not the next how-to-get-rich-quick-scheme. It's not going to tell you 101 ways to book new parties, how to recruit a million into your downline, or give you 99 party themes to double your sales. It's MORE THAN SALES... a chronicle of the way you may feel while in direct sales; the doubts you have, problems you encounter, and the biblical answers that will propel you into the businesswoman God desires you to be.

It's also not about religion. It's about our businesses, our decisions, our feelings, and aligning those with the heart of our Creator... The One who knows us better than we know ourselves. My prayer is that even if you've never stepped foot in church or don't know Jesus as your personal Savior, this book will reach down into your very soul. Speak to you. Breathe in you. Believe in you. And bring you that much closer to the woman God has created you to be.

Each devotion is designed with a verse, a story, a time for reflection, and a prayer. Confession: the prayer was quite possibly the hardest part for me. Why? Because I've never read anyone else's prayer when it's included in a devotion. It's as if it's their prayer, not mine–it doesn't feel sincere if I'm just speaking someone else's words. I want to let you know you don't have to say these prayers word for word–they've come from *my* heart, as an offering to *my* God. If your prayers to God are different, it's okay. God wants our sincerity when we pray. The unprettiest prayer with all the "wrong" words is beautiful to the ears of Christ. Rest assured, God adores them AND you.

With Love,
Karen

In the Beginning

Day 1
What's In Your Kit?

> "A psalm of Solomon. Unless the LORD builds a house, the work of the builders is wasted. Unless the LORD protects a city, guarding it with sentries will do no good" (Psalm 127:1, NLT).

Whether you work from home or this is a second (or third!) job, whether you're a full-time representative, or a part-time hobbyist, you have a new business! Congratulations!

You more than likely purchased a starter kit to show your friends and get yourself going. What came in your kit? Did you get products? Order forms? Paper work? A how-to-guide? Maybe a login for an online presence? All of the above?

When we open our kit, we have all of the things we need to get us started in our business. How do we as Christians ensure that even with all of these things to help us succeed, our daily efforts aren't fruitless? By entering into a business partnership with the Lord! Psalm 127:1 (NIV) says,

> "Unless the Lord builds a house, the workers labor in vain."

Your house can be your life, your marriage, your family, or your job. See, you probably didn't think of God being in your kit, did you? Even if your Direct Sales company is a faith-based company, I'm sure the company didn't package God along with your startup investment.

"Oooo, look! I got three shades of lipstick, four eyeshadows and a baby Jesus! Yes!!"

But God is in our kit; do you know why? Because as Christians, all of the work we do here on earth is representative of Christ. People watch us for examples of how to act, react, and live on a daily basis, even if we don't realize it. Our businesses are no different. Whatever we speak about, work in, or represent our businesses in, God is a part of that.

Sometimes we jump into our businesses without seeking God's thoughts, or without praying about it. Sometimes we spend weeks or months in prayer. I have friends who prayed for months, while I was that girl who signed up on a whim. If you didn't pray about it, don't feel bad or stress out–I'm not here to judge! Even if you didn't pray for months in advance, you can still ask God to be your business partner from this point forward.

Back to our verse. "Unless the Lord builds the house, the workers labor in vain." If He doesn't build it and our efforts are useless, what's the flip-side of that? That if the Lord DOES build the house, it WILL be blessed and it WILL flourish! Isn't that what we want for our businesses? Even if we didn't ask God before jumping into our venture at the start, we can always align our businesses with His vision *now* to ask for His help to build our house!

Now here's the cool thing: If God has a vested interest in our business because it's HIS business too, wouldn't HE want it to succeed? Sure would!

I believe we all want our businesses to be successful! We want them to flourish, to thrive, and to accomplish the underlying goals we had when we first entertained the thought of joining our companies. But how much better will it be with God's hand of blessing on it? How much **more** can you accomplish for yourself, your family, and for God if you have His help? **Take God out of your kit and make Him your active business partner!**

~ Think About It ~

Is my house prospering? Or is my labor in vain? Is God truly building my house, or did I take the blueprints out of his hands because my way is better and faster?

_____

_____

_____

_____

_____

_____

If God is building your house, thank Him for all He has done. If you've taken that control away from Him, can you give it back to Him?

~ Pray About It ~

Precious heavenly father, thank you so much for this business you've given me. I can't do it alone–I don't WANT to do it alone. I need your guidance, your ear, your hand to help make this business a success. I ask you to help me build this house. I may not always understand what you're doing, but I give this business to you, and ask that you remind me that you ARE the builder of this house when I do try to take that control back. I lay this business down as an offering to you, and ask that you help me grow it to provide for myself, my family, and for you. Help me make it all you want it to be, without limiting it to my own imagination. Thank you Lord for being my business partner. ~ Amen

~

Now be excited; you just made GOD your business partner! The one who created the earth and everything in it! Woo hooo!!

Day 2
Family Matters–
Changing Your Dynamic

"At dusk, when it was time to close the city gate, they left. I don't know which way they went. Go after them quickly. You may catch up with them" (Joshua 2:5, NIV).

Despite having a good college education, and a really well-paying job, our family was struggling financially. We didn't just live paycheck to paycheck, it was worse than that! With no reserves in the bank, if an unexpected bill or situation came up, we had to borrow money to cover it. Family members were envious of our house, or cars (no, those things weren't extravagant, but still more than they had), but all I saw when I looked at the *things* we had was another hour I'd have to work to make the payment for it. Sadly, there was just no end in sight.

When the direct sales opportunity came to me, I didn't just see a paycheck, I saw freedom. Freedom from debt. Freedom from a job I didn't like but had to keep to pay the bills. (It's a vicious cycle, isn't it?) Freedom from worrying about how I was going to make the next payment, and freedom to work from home and be a good mother for my kids as they start reaching the age where peer pressure leads them down a path I don't want them to take.

So I jumped. I didn't know anything about direct sales. I was an introvert, not a salesperson, and I'll be honest, I didn't know how I was going to sell handbags. Ninety percent of the time, I stuffed everything I owned into my pockets and called it a day. But I needed to change our family dynamic, and I felt positive this was a way I could do that.

Have you ever felt there was something out there that could change your whole life if you took a chance? Rahab did. She was a prostitute living in Jericho, whose home was built into the city walls. (At that time, the walls of the city were so thick that a home could be built into it, thus fortifying the city and ensuring its protection from invaders.)

After the Jews (followers of God) had escaped from slavery, followed God into the desert, and wandered there for 40 years they finally entered the Promised Land of Canaan. Their original leader, Moses, had died, and now they were being led by Joshua, who was a mighty warrior. God had told the Jews that Jericho would be theirs, and He would help them capture it, so Joshua sent two spies to scope out the land. They were spotted, which sent the city into fear, and they beat on Rahab's door until she let them in.

Now why would you think the city would be in fear over two men? It's because GOD was on their side, and the people of Jericho KNEW it! The Israelites had conquered every other city in their path, and NOW these two men were in Jericho. God hadn't failed them yet. If these men were now in YOUR town, wouldn't you be scared?

Rahab let these two strangers that were pounding on her door into her home, but here's the thing. She *knew* who they were. They weren't strangers. No, she'd never met them, but she'd heard of them. And unfortunately, the king of Jericho knew who *she* was, and that she'd helped them. He sent this message to Rahab:

> "Bring out the men who came to you and entered your house, because they have come to spy out the whole land" (Joshua 2:3).

But the woman had taken the two men and hidden them.

> She said, "Yes, the men came to me, but I did not know where they had come from. At dusk, when it was time to close the city gate, they left. I don't know which way they went. Go after them quickly. You may catch up with them" (Joshua 2:4-5).

Rahab blatantly lied to the king when she told him she didn't know where the spies were. She knew exactly where they were because she let them escape through her roof! She said to them in Joshua 11:9, 11:

> "I know that the Lord has given you this land and that a great fear of you has fallen on us, so that all who live in this country are melting in fear because of you... When we heard of it, our hearts melted in fear and everyone's courage failed because of you, for the Lord your God is God in heaven above and on the earth below."

She made an oath with them to spare her family in return for her showing favor to them, and not turning them in. She would keep silent, knowing they were coming back to wipe out the city, in exchange for her family's safety. She would hang a scarlet cord from her window so that when they saw it, the Israelites would bypass her and keep her safe.

You see, Rahab knew what would happen to her city. It had happened to others! But rather than run scared like the king and everyone else, Rahab chose to FOLLOW God. She didn't know this God as her own yet. But she knew of His power, she knew what He'd done for those who DID follow him, and she wanted to be with those people. She knew he was the one true God, and she was willing to risk her own

20

life and the lives of her family to make sure she could be included in with the Jews.

When Rahab purposely sent the king's spies in the opposite direction of the two Jews, she saw an opportunity to change her family's dynamic. She saw an opportunity for mercy and grace, and to save her family in a situation that was hopeless for everyone else. Because of her faith, Rahab not only saved her life, but she also saved her family's lives as well. Later, because of her faith, Rahab married one of the spies she sheltered and would be in the very lineage of Jesus![1] That's proof positive you don't have to be perfect or have a perfect history to change the world. The Bible is full of imperfect people who took the hand of Jesus and walked into their destiny. Will you take His hand and walk into yours?

~ Think About It ~

Is this business opportunity a chance to change your family's dynamic? It doesn't have to be money. You can be the first to go to college, the first to own a home, or the first to get to attend your kids' sporting events when your family didn't even have the money or means for you to DO the events as a kid, let alone attend. MAYBE your mission is to use this business to change someone ELSE'S dynamic–a team mate, a party guest, or even children in another country–when you bless them with something that sprouted from this business. Where is God asking you to follow or trust Him? What is God's life-changing opportunity for you in this business?

_____

_____

_____

_____

_____

_____

~ Pray About It ~

Lord Jesus, I want to be Rahab. I want to take this business and have it change my dynamic, my family's dynamic, and the dynamic of women I don't even know yet. I want you to take the life that I am living, and help me see how this business can be with YOU holding the reigns. Give me wisdom to know the opportunity when I see it, because your word says when anyone asks for wisdom, you will give it to them. I thank you so much for the plans you have for me, and ask that you will help me stay the course when I can't see the change yet. Thank you, Lord, that YOU care enough about me to even give me the chance to change my family's dynamic and be as Rahab–saved by your grace and capable of taking a leap of faith that will change generations. ~ Amen.

Day 3
Blessed Be the Naysayers, for They Shall Inherit a Closet Full of Products

"When the Pharisees saw this, they asked his disciples, 'Why does your teacher eat with tax collectors and sinners?'"(Matthew 9:11, NIV).

I remember when I first told my husband I was going to sell purses to make a little extra cash each month. Of course there was laughter (which was NOT, in that case, the best medicine). There was some distinct eye rolling, followed by "You're going to do what? Isn't that a pyramid scheme?" There was skepticism, more laughter, and patronizing cliches like: "You know you won't make any money," "Who's going to buy all this stuff," and "This better not cost us any money."

Some direct sales professionals are lucky to have a ready-made cheerleading section. I was not only going to have to tell myself why I was doing this each time I went to a party or talked about it, I would also now have to hear from the peanut gallery at home about what a scam direct sales was, and how I'd better not quit my day job. After all, it isn't a "real" job that could provide for our family, and there is no respect in the profession. Have mercy.

Do you have a naysayer in your life?

Jesus had naysayers too. He had people who doubted Him, and people who questioned His work. In Matthew 9, when he first called Matthew to be a disciple, good old Matt was hanging out in the tax collector's booth. Jesus asked him to follow him, which Matthew did. Some time later, Jesus was eating supper with him when the Pharisees saw them, and asked his other disciples: "Dude. Why is your teacher hanging out with sinners and tax collectors?"

You see, Matthew was a tax collector by trade, and tax collectors were a hated bunch. In those days, they could walk up to a person and tax him for what they had in their pocket. People were taxed for their income, for property, things they bought, ate, drank, and even taxed for emergencies. Oh and get this— whatever the tax collectors gathered on top of the taxes, they could keep for themselves.

Now tell me that doesn't introduce a huge opportunity to take as much as you want from the common people in the name of "taxes", while pocketing whatever you can!

These tax collectors were usually fellow Jews who worked for Roman Gentiles, and thus were lumped in the same category: comparable to sinners and prostitutes. Yep, tax collector = prostitution.

Being with tax collectors and sinners lowered Jesus' credibility. It didn't matter to them that by giving up this profession to follow Jesus, Matthew was making a huge sacrifice. It just mattered that Jesus wasn't doing what the Pharisees thought he should.

You see, holiness in those days meant avoiding spending time with or eating with ungodly people. So here comes Jesus doing just that. What was he thinking? What kind of example was he setting? He was losing respect. The Bible doesn't clearly call out that there was eye-rolling, but you can see it, can't you? Those naysayers pointed out his actions with an incredulous "You're doing what?!"

Sound familiar?

Jesus tells us how we should respond to naysayers. He was not concerned with everyone else's idea of what he was to do. His concern was with God's ultimate plan for him to offer salvation to EVERYONE, sinners and tax collectors included, and for him to offer that, he had to be with those who would receive him, not just those he was supposed to hang with.

When we have naysayers, we can't be concerned with their thoughts of what's ideal for our life. Yes, just as was the case in Jesus' time, *sometimes* they're concerned for us and our reputation. But just like God's grace was bigger than the limitations the Pharisees had set on Jesus, His ultimate plan for us and what we can do with his business is bigger than the limitations our friends and family have set. And like Jesus, we also need to brush aside their comments and continue with the work we started... and maybe give the naysayer one of your company's products for every birthday, anniversary, and Christmas gift for the next 10 years. (wink, wink)

~ Think About It ~

Do you have a naysayer in your life? How have you responded to their comments? Have you responded angrily, hurtfully, or spitefully? Have you let the naysayers influence you to the point of pausing this new business venture? What one thing can you take away from Jesus' reaction to the naysayers to help grow your business?

_____

_____

_____

_____

_____

_____

~ Pray About It ~

Father God, I have some naysayers in my life. You know who they are. It's hard to be in a right mind about our business when I hear their words in the back of my mind telling me to give up. I don't want to give up, Lord. Please squash their words, and replace them with your words of confidence. Where I have a naysayer, please replace their words with someone who is encouraging to me. I believe your goal for me and our business is much greater than the limitations my friends and family have set for me. Help me to see that vision you have for me when the naysayers come, and speak so that I can hear your voice above all the rest. ~ Amen

Day 4
Fair-Weather Friends

"Then they sat on the ground with him for seven days and seven nights. No one said a word to him, because they saw how great his suffering was" (Job 2:13, NIV).

I have been so blessed to have some wonderful friends in my life. Some of my friends have been friends since high school, some even since elementary school! Whether from church, past neighborhoods, or direct sales connections, I couldn't imagine my life without any of these amazing women in it.

I have two friends in particular, both have been my friends for a good 20+ years. In school, we were the three musketeers. One has joined my direct sales business, and the other has not. I love that I can work alongside one friend in our business ventures and encourage her along her journey. However, the friend who has not joined is still one of my very best friends, and I truly love her with all my heart. Because she doesn't have the same opportunities to combine work with pleasure, I have to make time to be with her. Not just because she is my friend, but because time with her is worth it!

It can be tempting when we spend so much of our time on our business to congregate with friends just from direct sales. Sometimes, those acquaintances we meet through our businesses can become best friends just based on the amount of time we spend with them and on shared goals and experiences. They can drive you, push you, and celebrate with you! Admittedly, that can leave our friends who aren't in direct sales with us in the dust, feeling neglected! Throughout your journey, it's important to recognize the people that God has placed in your life both INSIDE and OUTSIDE of your direct sales business! True friendship transcends career choices, and makes sure the people we love are part of our lives even if our direct sales business isn't a consideration.

Take Job for instance. Job was a great guy. He was successful, had a great business, with herds of cattle, sheep, and camels. He loved God, and was a righteous man. He had a loving family with ten children. The Bible describes Job as the greatest man in the east! Satan came to God one day and said "I bet if you took all of that away, you'd find out the true character of your so-called follower, Job." God allowed Satan to take any of Job's possessions away, as long as Job himself was not killed. One by one, Job's things were snatched up from him. His herds. His belongings. His home. His children. Satan even took Job's personal health, hoping that Job would curse the name of God.

But Job didn't.

When all of his things were taken away, and Job was left with nothing, he still couldn't curse God. And that was when his friends stepped in. Eliphaz, Bildad, and Zophar met and agreed they would go comfort Job. Now those are some true friends. He couldn't take them out to dinner to chat. Couldn't meet over coffee. Couldn't give them a sheep for traveling to see them. They came anyway, to his rescue. Job 2:12 says,

> "They saw him from a distance and wept over him."

They mourned with him. And for seven days and seven nights, they sat on the ground with him, sharing in his mourning, not saying a word. What a true picture of friendship! They weren't friends with him because he had high sales and they wanted to be a part of that. They weren't friends because he'd earned a leadership trip and they wanted to go with him. They were friends in his darkest hour, when he had nothing to give in return. They sat with him. They mourned with him. They loved on him and empathized with him the way God tells us to love one another.

Only you and God know what's behind the heart of *your* friendships. Make sure that they aren't based solely on the success of your business. As women, we love having other women encourage and celebrate with us. But direct sales can go through cycles as well, so choose friends that can also sit in the dirt and cry with you like Eliphaz, Bildad, and Zophar did for their friend Job. Use caution not to neglect your friends who aren't in direct sales as you start your new venture. As the saying goes, "Make new friends, but keep the old. One is silver and the other's gold."

Sometimes even friends who are in the same business will part ways for a bit. In one direct sales business that I worked in, a friend and I seemed to be on the same journey for a long time, then our journey came to a fork in the road. My heart was broken, because she didn't return calls or messages, or even texts, for days! It was hurtful, because I thought she'd become one of my best friends. Yes, she was a friend for one leg of my journey, but looking back, I can see how God separated us and why. The fork that she took wasn't a path I needed to travel with her. I was so thankful though, because I had great friends who were providing Godly counsel in the meantime. Had I continued on the path with her, I may have missed out on the wonderful new friendships God opened up instead.

~ Think About It ~

What about you? Is there someone in your life that may not be giving you Godly counsel for your business, or may be taking you down the wrong business path? Proverbs 17:7 says,

> "Iron sharpens iron, and one man sharpens another."

Do you need to continue down the path with her, helping each other become better women, or is God calling you to take the other path from the fork in the road? Is there a friend you've neglected because she wasn't in direct sales that you need to make time for? God knows we need friends—even Jesus says in John 15:12-15,

> "This is my commandment, that you love one another as I have loved you. Greater love has no one than this, that someone lay down his life for his friends. You are my friends if you do what I command you. No longer do I call you servants, for the servant does not know what his master is doing; but I have called you friends, for all that I have heard from my Father I have made known to you."

Be honest—is there a person in your life who has ousted you from theirs since you started your business? Was it because when you see them, all you talk about is your latest cooking utensil, necklace, or tote bag from your company, making her feel like a walking checkbook instead of a friend?

_____

_____

_____

_____

_____

_____

~ Pray About It ~

Lord, thank you for the friends you've placed in my life. Thank you that we aren't here on this earth alone. For those women that have become my true friends, both within this business and outside of it, I am so thankful you've entrusted their friendships to me. Lord, thank you for placing the women I've needed at the exact time in my life to help me grow as a woman, not just as a businesswoman. Help me see the women in MY life who need me to be their friend, so that I can share in the ups and downs of their life the way my friends have shared in those moments with me, and help me remember my friends are friends, not checkbooks. Help me know who is a true friend, and who I can trust to sit in the dirt. Above all, thank you Lord that YOU are a true friend to me, listening when I need an ear, guiding my life, my business, and walking this life with me in both good times and bad. Thank you Jesus... for friends.

Day 5
Overcoming Fears to Grow Your Business

"And her husband Joseph, being a just man and unwilling to put her to shame, resolved to divorce her quietly" (Matthew 1:19, ESV).

If you've never felt fear in your direct sales business, stop right where you are, and give thanks to God! (Don't worry, I'll just wait here.) Fear can manifest itself and take on many forms, from being afraid to ask for parties to get started, to being afraid to upsell. It can be fear when you aren't meeting your minimum and are about to go inactive, or fear to talk to an upline, downline, or angry client–even fear of providing for your family.

Fear is stifling, and if you succumb to it, it can bring your business to a screeching halt. There are times we simply have no choice but to overcome that fear to grow our business–or else. And it seems so easy for someone else to say to you "Don't worry, it'll work out." Maybe it did–for them. But they're not in your shoes. They don't have your bills, they don't have your customers, and they don't have your empty calendar.

Every fear you have is a whisper from the devil. Where God says "Trust Me", Satan whispers "But it never worked before."

Where God says "Talk to that lady over there," Satan whispers "Nah, not her. She won't like your product."

Where God says "Call your client, tell her the truth and apologize–she'll be a client for life," Satan says "Do it tomorrow. Better yet, she's probably forgotten anyway, and your apology will just dig up an old wound. Just let it go."

We listen to the whisper of Satan, allowing fear to stifle our business by telling us we can't, instead of listening to the voice of God tell us to fearlessly try.

Joe was afraid too, at first. You see, Joe's fiancé was pregnant, and it wasn't his baby. They promised each other they would wait until their wedding day to make love, but her infidelity is unforgivable. How could he be with a woman who won't even stay faithful to him before they're married? Heartache, anger, betrayal–how could she? Surely they can't go walking down the aisle with the baby bump showing—everyone knows the date of their wedding, and the plans they've made. She is a nut case through and through–(even says the baby is GOD'S baby, and He's the real father), so it's probably best he get out while he can anyway. Joe plans to quietly leave her–in fact where Joe lives, a divorce, separation, or being an unwed mother are all scarlet letters. But infidelity is acceptable grounds for divorce. Leaving her would clear his own conscience, and doing so quietly would make sure she isn't flogged. Win all around, right?

But God had other plans for Joe–rather, Joseph–the earthly father of Jesus. Matthew 1 says,

> "And her husband Joseph, being a just man and unwilling to put her to shame, resolved to divorce her quietly. But as he considered these things, behold, an angel of the Lord appeared to him in a dream, saying, "Joseph, son of David, do not fear to take Mary as your wife, for that which is conceived in her is from the Holy Spirit. She will bear a son, and you shall call his name Jesus, for he will save his people from their sins." All this took place to fulfill what the Lord had spoken by the prophet: "Behold, the virgin shall conceive and bear a son, and they shall call his name Immanuel" (which means, God with us). When Joseph woke from sleep, he did as the angel of the Lord commanded him: he took his wife, but knew her not until she had given birth to a son. And he called his name Jesus."

This whole situation was a nightmare for Joseph; what would society think of him, either way? Joe went from feeling apprehensive and fearful about marrying a crazy, unfaithful woman to hearing that she really wasn't crazy, and he would have a whole new set of fears to overcome. *How can I raise a child who is directly from the Holy Spirit? I'm not worthy! What do I do? What do I say to people who ask why she is pregnant before we're even married?!*

But Joseph HAD to overcome these fears to move forward with the plan God had already set in motion. Standing still was not an option. Hearing confirmation that this really was God's plan was just what he needed to overcome his fears with Mary, the mother of Jesus. He knew that if God SET this path for him, God would STAY ON THIS PATH WITH HIM for the duration.

~ Think About It ~

What if you truly believed that God set this path for you? I think you want to, or you wouldn't be here reading with me. By staying afraid, we can never go from where we are, to where God wants us to be.

If Joseph had given in to that fear, Mary would have been a single, unwed mother. But God knew Joseph was a good man, and knew he was the father Jesus needed here on earth. Likewise, GOD BELIEVES IN YOU. He entrusts YOU with things that only you can accomplish as well. He is waiting for you to realize that He has your back, and would not set you on a path unless He plans to walk it with you. He is waiting on YOU. What are you waiting for? Take the step you need, knowing He is with you the same way he was with Joseph.

_____

_____

_____

_____

_____

_____

~ Pray About It ~

Father God, I think so many times that I am on this journey alone, and I forget you're here with me, helping me work this business. Give me peace to know THIS IS MY JOURNEY, and that you are right here, already clearing the path for me, and waiting for me to take the first step. Give me strength to lift my foot to take that step, then strength to take another, and freedom to take off and run! Thank you Lord for your hand on my business, and forgive me when I come back to you in one day, or two days, or three to check back and make sure this path is still okay. Give me faith without a shadow of a doubt that will help me overcome EVERY fear. ~ Amen.

More Than Sales

THE JESUS-MINDED
BUSINESS PERSON

Day 6
Order Amongst Chaos

When I sent this book and each day's topic over to my sweet friend and editor, I told her it was complete, but seemed to be missing something. What, I couldn't put my finger on exactly. She reminded me that God is a God of order, and maybe we needed a day to focus on that. I had to laugh.

You see, as hard as I try to *be 100%* organized, it just doesn't happen. I am a planner addict, usually buying 3-4 planners per year because none of them can organize my life perfectly. Yes, look in my spice cabinet and everything is organized by size and frequency of use. But look in my dresser drawer and you'll find 47 unmatched socks mixed in with shirts, in with Mother's Day cards from the past 2 years, and one extra battery for the smoke detector.

When it comes to my business, I am 100% certain I have at least 10 different locations in my home that are housing the current season's catalog. Surely, God wouldn't expect me–the one who is more organized chaos than true order–to tell everyone else how to live a life organized, right?

But that's just it. God IS a God of order. Think about it. 1 Corinthians 14:40 says,

> "But all things should be done decently and in order."

And then God reminds me that *you* aren't looking at *me* for perfection, you're looking at *HIM*. Think about all God has done for a specific purpose. None of it was willy-nilly. The way that God created the earth, in a certain order of operations. The way He gave Noah explicit instructions for building an ark. How He spent 16 chapters of Exodus explaining in great detail the smallest dimensions, materials, and requirements for His temple. Order matters to God.

In Mark 6, when Jesus was feeding a crowd with bread and fish, vs 6:39-41 tells us,

> "Then he commanded them all to sit down in groups on the green grass. So they sat down in groups, by hundreds and by fifties. And taking the five loaves and the two fish he looked up to heaven and said a blessing and broke the loaves and gave them to the disciples to set before the people. And he divided the two fish among them all."

More Than Sales

Everything God breathes upon IS ordered. Guess what? That includes you and me. When God created us in His own image, that meant we were designed with the ABILITY to be like Christ.
Huh?

Let me explain. It doesn't mean we'll ever be as great as God, be perfect, or even be worthy to speak the name of the one who created the heavens. What it does mean is that the ability to BE organized, because we are made in God's image and He IS a God of order, is already within us! We just have to develop it!

The individual personalities that God gave us all allows us to take the *idea* of order and make it our own. That means some leaders may use colored index cards to keep track of their hostesses, while others use an app. Some may use a 3-ring binder while others use a disc system to keep track of order forms or team members' birthdates. But to say we aren't organized or can't *be* organized takes credit away from the very one who plants the seed of organization within us!

I say yes, you can be organized. You simply have to find the system that works for you. Remember, we are in a business partnership with our Lord! He left explicit instructions on what we should do while He's away from the office.

Matthew 25 tells about three servants who were given business holdings to look after while the Master was away. One of the servants wisely invested it, and made double the return on his investment.

Another servant did the same. The Master was so pleased with how they ran the business while he was away that he made them business partners!

The third servant didn't have a clue what to do with the money. He took the lazy way out, and instead of finding a system that would work, he simply said "Well, I thought I would just tuck it away since that's what *you* probably wanted anyway."

God doesn't want to be short-changed and He doesn't want you to be either! He's given you authority over this business. When He asks you how you're doing, you can respond in one of two ways– either you are flourishing, taking small risks that should pay off in the end and everything is running as planned, or you're playing it safe with a half-hearted attempt to run a business.

Now I know what you're thinking. *Karen, you have totally veered off topic. What does organization have to do with the servants who invested the Master's money?* My answer is this: everything.

To run a good–no, great–business, you must be organized. You have to have a system to know your team, your customers, your products, and your money. You would expect nothing less out of a small local business, right? You'd want them to know their staff and treat them well. You'd want them to be friendly, make conversation with you, and if you shop frequently, to recognize you and know you by name. You'd also expect them to know what products they have and have the ability to make recommendations for a product that could solve a need that you have. And you'd want to make sure they didn't mismanage your funds if you ordered a product that you didn't take home that day. They wouldn't be able to do any of this for you if they weren't organized.

I can't tell you what the perfect system will be for you to help you know the exact heartbeat of your business. Maybe it's that perfect planner with inventory and product sections, your booking calendar, a money app, and a simple looseleaf sheet in a binder for each girl in your downline that you update each time you talk with her. Maybe it's a color-coded marker system, a small bookcase full of displayed products, catalogs, order forms, and hostess cards, or a perfectly organized office without a speck of dust in the air. That's between you and God to develop the best way to keep your preferred style and still maintain a heavenly order about your business.

If you ask Him, he'll help you find the best way. His word tells us that He doesn't withhold wisdom from anyone who asks, and that includes wisdom on how to run a business and keep it organized. They don't have to be expensive or elaborate systems–I've seen near-miracles worked with a hall linen closet! They don't have to be pretty, or even all in one area. But you do need to get them started, one area at a time.

~ Think About It ~

We may not ever organize our top sock drawers. Our businesses, however, need that organization to feed our families, pay our bills, and sow seed back into the kingdom. Organization and order can ensure we have a no-fail method of keeping track of the most important areas of our business, and make sure we have an amazing return on our invested kit money. Is there one area you can think of right now that could use a little more order? Is it a way to thank your customers, or a way to categorize your products on hand, or even a way to record your mileage for taxes? Don't look around and see the things that aren't perfect. Choose one area each day that needs improvement, and begin injecting order into chaos this week!

_____

_____

_____

_____

_____

_____

~ Pray About It ~

Father God, thank you so much for giving me the ability to be organized. But more importantly, thank you for making me unique, not like a robot, allowing me to use my own gifts and abilities to find the best way to stay organized in all that I do. Thank you for the faith you have in ME, Lord Jesus, to be the business owner you know I can be. In Your precious, holy name, Amen.

Day 7

Tithing & Giving

> "Honor the LORD with your possessions, and with the first fruits of all your increase; so your barns will be filled with plenty, and your vats will overflow with new wine" (Proverbs 3:9-10, NKJV).

Many an argument has been had over tithing–how much, when, to whom, and why. Some churches make their members pledge a certain amount, while others require members to bring in a tax statement to ensure they're tithing as the church believes they should. I can't tell you what's right for you and your business, but I can tell you what God's heart was for *mine*.

You see, it's hard to tell a woman on your team who isn't making ends meet to begin with that she has to give 10% off the top to God, when that 10% may mean formula and diapers for her babies. I'm not going to tell you that. In the Old Testament, the law was very much cut and dried–give out of thanks for blessings already received, as Abram and Jacob did, give to support the priests, and give to learn respect and reverence for God. It was the first fruit, to be given before anything else was paid. The New Testament shares a different viewpoint. When Paul talks to the church in Corinth, he tells them that they should set aside a sum of money at the beginning of the week

"...as God hath prospered him,"

for the saints. In 2 Corinthians 8, he goes on to tell them about the Macedonians, who gave with great joy, even though they were poor! They felt it was their privilege to give, and they did so not because it was a required 10%, but because they loved the Lord. They recognized that their blessings came from Him, and wanted to honor him joyfully, by giving back to Him! In verse 12, he tells the Corinthians

> "For if the willingness is there, the gift is acceptable according to what one has, not according to what he does not have."

If your check is written every commission run, but you aren't giving to the Lord joyfully, the gift isn't acceptable!

God doesn't want our gifts back to Him, and our service to Him to be a checkbox on our weekly Christianity to-do list. He's not a mafia boss looking for His cut, or a bully shaking you down for your lunch money every day. God doesn't *need* your money! He has infinite funds and an infinite means to get

them. In fact, money is no consequence to Him at all–
He can accomplish everything He needs to do without
it. Rather, God wants you to give to Him because you
want to!

Giving to God shows Him that we truly
believe He is in charge of our finances, and that we
trust Him to provide for us. When we don't use all of
our income, we move from *saying* we trust Him to
actually trusting Him! Malachi 3:10 says,

> "Bring the whole tithe into the
> storehouse, that there may be food in my
> house. Test me in this," says the LORD
> Almighty, "and see if I will not throw
> open the floodgates of heaven and pour
> out so much blessing that you will not
> have room enough for it."

See, that trust flows two ways. If God knows
that He can trust us with funds, He's going to keep
giving us more! He will throw open the floodgates are
rain down on us–so much that you won't even have
room for it! But we have to be trustworthy too! Luke
16:10 says,

> "Whoever can be trusted with very little
> can also be trusted with much, and
> whoever is dishonest with very little will
> also be dishonest with much."

More Than Sales

If God knows that what He gives us will be given back, and not squandered or wasted, He'll entrust us with more of that. We're a good return on His investment!

But here's the kicker: He wants us to WANT to give back to Him. Not because we'll get it returned to us or out of fear. Out of love. Joyfully. And here's the other thing–not just money–He wants you to give of yourself! Time, abilities, sharing your talents with others who can't repay you, and sharing your leadership abilities with others who may not have or know their leaders.

One night, I was wide awake, worried about the health of my business. I was "Facebook friends" with an upper level leader. We had never met, but she mentioned something in a group page that had me wondering, so I reached out and sent her a message. She wasn't my upline, and she earns no money off of me, but that woman replied. She reached out to me, counseled me, and advised me until 2 am! And then, she prayed with me. Her selfless giving had such an impact on my own business and the way I treated others from that point forward–both those on my team and those outside of it. Giving money does not honor God if a consultant in need comes to you with a problem that your God-given talents or abilities could solve, and you shun or ignore her. While you may not say it verbally, your actions clearly say that your own success is the only one that matters.

Let's be clear—I'm not asking you to take on every woman's business as your own—that's impossible. My friend Mary had nothing to gain—in fact, she probably wouldn't even recognize me on the street—but her sacrifice of time and talent was an offering not just to me, but to God! He honors sacrifice and giving with a grateful, thankful heart, in all its forms—giving money, and giving time or talents. Taking a minute to help someone who may not be able to help you speaks directly to God's heart. When we give back what has been given to us, we put our businesses back in His hands. This proves to Him that we not only trust Him, but that He can trust us in return.

~ Think About It ~

There's a big difference between tithing because you have to, and giving because you want to. Giving implies no expectations—it's a gift that needn't ever be returned, yet God always *does* return it—tenfold! Are you tithing, or giving? If you're giving, are you giving money, or of ALL of your talents, abilities, time, and leadership? Who can you think of that immediately comes to mind when you think of sharing your talents and leadership insights and abilities with them?

_____

_____

_____

_____

More Than Sales

~ Pray About It ~

Dear Jesus, thank you so much for blessing my business now, and for the future blessings to come. Help me remember that ALL of my success is in your hands–that a simple breath from you can help me succeed or fail. I trust you to take care of my business, and I want to give freely, without concern if those funds will be replaced. I trust you, and I trust that you will help me see only whom to give to, not the hit my checkbook will take. Help me see the women you have in mind for me to share my time, gifts, and talents to help them grow THEIR businesses as well. Thank you Lord that You have chosen to entrust these funds to me, and I pray that I honor you in the way I return them. ~Amen

Day 8
Being Still

"Find a quiet, secluded place so you won't be tempted to role-play before God. Just be there as simply and honestly as you can manage. The focus will shift from you to God, and you will begin to sense His grace" (Matthew 6:6, MSG).

Sometimes we can get so busy doing things for our kids, our spouses, our upline, our teams, and our businesses, that we forget about ourselves. Things are due for school, the dog needs shots, a work project is overdue by a week at your day job, your husband is giving you that "come hither" look every time you turn around, and one of your colleagues keeps giving you the stink-eye whenever you mention your latest adventure in your business. Before you know it, you can end up burnt out and ready to fly the coop altogether! What's a girl to do?

The answer is simple: Nothing.

You see, when Jesus was troubled, stressed, or just needed to gather His thoughts, he did nothing! By nothing, I mean he retreated. He got alone, in the still and quiet, with just God. He prayed and rested, and sought God's answers to His needs.

> Mark 1:35 says, "Very early in the morning, while it was still dark, Jesus got up, left the house and **went off to a solitary place**, where he prayed."

> Mark 6:45-46 says, "And immediately He made His disciples get into the boat and go ahead of Him to the other side to Bethsaida, while He Himself was sending the multitude away. **And after bidding them farewell, he departed** to the mountain to pray."

> And Luke 5:16 says, "But He Himself **would often slip away** to the wilderness and pray."

When Jesus heard of the death of John the Baptist, He once again left to be alone and pray. After He fed the 5,000, He left to be alone and pray. Jesus could have handled ANYTHING–He was God's son! There was no task that was beyond His reach, yet He took time often to retreat in peace and quiet to seek the heart of His father!

Why then, do we think WE are so invincible that we can't take time for ourselves to rest and be still?

You see, many of the Jesus' disciples had gathered around him to tell them everything they had going on. There were people everywhere, each trying to report in what they'd done, and who they'd taught. They were so busy they never even had a chance to sit down and eat! His answer to them was to go away. Rather, to go away to a quiet place with Him, and be still.

Yes, God does give us work to do here on earth, but Jesus' example for us is to both work AND rest. In fact, one of the first examples to rest and Be Still was in Genesis! When God created the heavens and the earth, He rested on the 7th day. WE are made in His image–crafted in His mind, after His heart–if He had to rest, wouldn't we?

I want to tell you that it's more complex than that–that to carve out time for yourself you have to look at your calendar and work your business 35% of your day, and of that, 25% should be building your business, with the remaining 75% building your team, but I'm not here to tell you how to run your business. I am here to tell you God's *heart* for your business, and that is completely different.

Business experts will tell you one thing–to draw on others, to surround yourself with those who are higher than you are, or to only work around those who are "winners." God's heart is for you to work wholeheartedly as unto Him, and take time to rest when it's time to rest. He wants you to walk barefoot with Him in the garden, the way He did with Adam and Eve–but guess what? We can't walk barefoot in the garden when we always have our running shoes on! We can't rest, be still, and actively seek His heart until we **stop talking** long enough to hear Him!

> Matthew 11:28-30 tells us that Jesus says, "Come to Me, all who are weary and heavy-laden, and I will give you rest. Take My yoke upon you, and learn from Me, for I am gentle and humble in heart; and you shall find rest for your souls. For My yoke is easy, and My load is light."

No matter how busy our schedules are, no matter how many jobs we have or hats we wear, God *wants* us to give Him our burdens and come to Him for rest. And when we do, we must also be willing to stop moving long enough to wait for His reply!

~ Think About It ~

We'll never hear God's heart for us if we're the ones doing all the talking, just as we'll never find rest in our business unless we *take it.* Work is to provide us with income, feed us, allow us to tithe, and provide for others, but never should we be so consumed with the many tasks that we have to do that we don't carve time out to rest with our Savior.

Do you have a set time each day that you rest and seek God? When life gets busy and you need to get away, do you seek refuge in the quiet place with God, or are you seeking something else to bring you rest? Realize that there is no peace for the soul like the peace that God can bring you when you seek Him! Are you reading the fullness of His word each day, getting bread and meat to sustain you, or are you sipping water and eating simple appetizers via the verse of the day app on your phone? He wants your WHOLE heart. He wants you to jump feet first into the pool of His goodness, not just dip your toe in the water so your clothes don't get wet. Go deeper. Trust me, the water's fine.

_____

_____

_____

_____

_____

_____

~ Pray About It ~

Dear Lord, I confess, sometimes I go all day without seeking you. I tell myself I'm busy, and my best time to talk to you is on the way to work, or in the afternoon, or on the way home, or before I go to bed. And the truth is, when that time comes that I promised to meet you, I am still too busy for more

More Than Sales

than a 5 minute speed-chat. I brush my quiet time aside until crisis mode sets in and a leisurely walk through the garden with you is long overdue. Days, weeks, months between true quiet time with you is set aside because my schedule and priorities are out of whack. Lord, forgive me for not making time to be still with you. Remind me that in the midst of my busyness, adding this business to my life, that my days will run smoother with you than they ever will without you. Remind me that moments spent seeking your heart will never return void. Remind me dearest Jesus that being still with you is the best place for me each and every day. In Your precious, holy name.

~Amen

Day 9
Multitasking Like Nobody's Business

"But few things are needed—or indeed only one. Mary has chosen what is better, and it will not be taken away from her" (Luke 10:42, NIV).

At one time, I had FOUR jobs, five if you count writing. I was involved in two Direct Sales businesses, one as a leader, and the other as a founding representative. We also have a vacation planning business that my husband and I run, and I was a full-time engineer. (Do I even need to add wife and mother of two to that list?!) How did I get involved in all these jobs? Well, they all paid for different things, and they were started for different reasons. I wasn't a glutton for punishment, but I'd told myself rather than working one to the best of my ability that would create the income of two jobs together, I could take on TWO (or three, or four) to create the income I needed, and everything would be fine!

Of course, you couldn't talk any sense into me. I told myself I *was* working my first direct sales business, but I wasn't. I half-heartedly "led" my team with my weekly phone calls and Facebook posts. With the rest of my time, I had multiple recruits in the other direct sales business, but never did a single, solitary party. It was chaos. One day, I was in a training group with some other direct sellers.[2] The coach asked us to simply close our eyes for 60 seconds. No note-taking. No talking. No thinking. Just breathing.

That 60 seconds felt like a literal eternity. It took 20 seconds for me just to tell myself to stop using that time to make lists of all I had to do! I realized how long it'd been since I was still. In the weeks following that revelation, I heard God telling me I needed to realign myself with HIS priorities. It was hard, because I kept wanting to take back those things I'd given up. But God's priorities and mine were the opposite. Where mine was Job 1, 2, 3, 4, and 5, His were 5, 2, 1, and 4, and job 3 wasn't in the picture at all!

As soon as I readjusted, the chaos ceased. I was amazed at how realigning my own desires with the heart of God allowed me to transform not just my business, but the harmony and balance in my LIFE. It also gave me the courage to reach out to my team and confess my struggles. The biggest thing I heard back? They were feeling the same way and had no idea that leaders could feel it too! What about you? Are you feeling overwhelmed with all the multitasking and multiple hat-wearing you do in your life? You may not have to give something up completely, but is God calling you to realign instead?

There was another gal who God asked to realign her priorities. Martha. As Jesus and his disciples were traveling, they came up to a village where a woman named Martha opened up her home to them. She also had a sister, named Mary. Jesus and the disciples came to visit them, teaching them and telling them about the Father. Mary sat at Jesus' feet, soaking up every word, while Martha prepared for the visitors. You know how it is when visitors come, don't you? You're cleaning, cooking, running next door to borrow another ingredient you need, hiding dirty laundry in a basket in the closet, scooping everything into a utility tote and tossing it in the garage... all the things that need to be done. And Martha was doing all of it!

And then there was her lazy sister Mary, not lifting a finger. Can you imagine the muttering under her breath Martha must have done? The dirty looks she'd shoot Mary's way? Just sitting there talking to the guests, leaving Martha to do EVERYTHING. Martha's to do list kept growing larger and larger, and it upset her until she couldn't take it anymore! She came to Jesus and asked, "Lord, don't you care that my sister has left me to do the work by myself? Tell her to help me!"

But Jesus let her know that her priorities and his weren't the same! He said in Luke 10:41 & 42,

More Than Sales

"Martha, Martha,...you are worried and upset about many things, but few things are needed—or really just one. Mary has chosen what is better, and it will not be taken away from her."

Martha came to Jesus asking him to make her lazy sister get up and help her work for the guests. Instead, He told her that she needed to have the same priorities that Mary had: to spend time with Him, and soak up what He had for her. Mary didn't experience the chaos that Martha felt, because she was right where she needed to be.

~ Think About It ~

Are you right where you need to be? Are your priorities aligned with God's priorities for your business and your life? Or are you so busy with things you *think* you should be doing, that you're missing out on the things you *really* should be doing, the direction God wants you to take, and the blessings He has waiting for you?

_____

_____

_____

_____

_____

_____

~ Pray About It ~

Dear Jesus, I don't know which way is up. I've got so many irons in the fire that I'm overwhelmed, and I have no idea which priority aligns with yours. Would you help me with that? Will you show me what I can lay down or give to others so that I can focus on the plan you have for me? Will you help me know what to lay down to keep myself from being so busy with my own advancement that I forget to do the work you've tasked me to do? Give me peace, joy, and comfort in following you, and letting something go, knowing that YOUR plans are better than any I could dream up. In your name, Amen.

More Than Sales

Day 10
The Lord Giveth...

> "Has no one returned to give praise to God except this foreigner? (Luke 11:18, NIV).

Call me crazy, but sometimes being on top of the mountain can make me feel farther from God than when I'm in the valley! Have you ever felt that way? As if you miss God, and you felt so much closer when you were going through a period of low sales, high team turnover, or zero bookings? And now that your calendar's full, and your sales are high, you feel alone? Yes, those high sales are great! But it can still feel as if God is... Missing.

Perhaps it's because from the valley, we are seeking God and His direction for our life constantly. But from the top of the mountain, we can feel as if we already have that direction, almost like we're a kid that just received that first training-wheel-free push on our bicycle. We pedal happily off into the sunset, but then once we arrive, we look around and there's no one there but us! Rest assured, God doesn't just live in the valley; He is right there with us—or wants to be—no matter where we are on our mountain!

James 1:17 says,

"Every good and perfect gift is from above, coming down from the Father of the heavenly lights, who does not change like shifting shadows. He chose to give us birth through the word of truth, that we might be a kind of first fruits of all He created."

The Message Bible says these good and perfect gifts are:

"rivers of light cascading down from the Father of Light. There is nothing deceitful in God, nothing two-faced, nothing fickle. He brought us to life using the true Word, showing us off as the crown of all his creatures."

The CROWN of everything he created?! Can you even imagine how much He loves you? When we've suffered or struggled, God's mercy is our gift to us, His biggest treasure. Absence of hard times doesn't mean he's left us, in fact, quite the opposite. It means He has just showered us–the crown of all His creatures–with an abundance of blessing, *just because.*

So how can you stay on top of the mountain, and ensure that while you're there, God is too? Well, one way is to be thankful for our blessings–for parties, for bookings, for sales, for our families and jobs–for

More Than Sales

every perfect gift. Have you ever given someone a gift and they didn't thank you? Maybe they forgot, or got busy, or maybe their "social media public thank you" didn't go through. But either way, you didn't get any thanks at all!

Jesus was on his way to Jerusalem, and traveling along the border between Samaria and Galilee. The Samaritans weren't God's people; they were people who lived in northern Israel. They were racially mixed with Jewish and pagan (no religion) ancestors, and did not practice mainstream Judaism, although they did worship Yahweh (God). The Samaritans were looked down upon by Jews because of their impure ancestry, as well as their beliefs, Samaritans and Jews normally did not hang out together, but as Jesus was traveling, he came across ten Samaritan men who had a skin disease called leprosy.

This highly contagious disease of the skin, nerves and tissues made normal townsfolk avoid them at all costs. They couldn't worship or be in the town around regular inhabitants and were often exiled to survive on their own however they could. And here were ten of them! Normally, you wouldn't see Jews and Samaritans hanging out together, but in this instance, their common yet unfortunate bond had brought them all together.

They stood at a distance and Luke 11:13-19 says they,

"called out in a loud voice, "Jesus, Master, have pity on us!" When he saw them, he said, "Go, show yourselves to the priests." And as they went, they were cleansed. One of them, when he saw he was healed, came back, praising God in a loud voice. He threw himself at Jesus' feet and thanked him—and he was a Samaritan.

Jesus asked, "Were not all ten cleansed? Where are the other nine? Has no one returned to give praise to God except this foreigner?" Then he said to him, "Rise and go; your faith has made you well."

There were ten that were healed by Jesus—nine were Jews—the churchgoers of today, and one was a Samaritan, maybe the one who doesn't go to church, or just listens to Christian music on the radio, and only HE was the one that came back to thank Jesus. Can you imagine how Jesus felt? That the people who are supposed to be closest to Him didn't even come back to thank Him?

I can tell you it is SO WONDERFUL to be in a place in our businesses and lives that is easy, where the good things are flowing, isn't it? But those are also the times when we sometimes forget to give God recognition for being the orchestrator of that!

~ Think About It ~

Are you that 10th Samaritan, routinely thanking God for His blessings on your business? Or are you one of the nine, that sometimes forgets? Knowing that God thinks of you as the crown of His creations, the pièce de résistance, do you have a hard time understanding that God WANTS to give you these good things? That He gives them to you not because of something you *did*, but simply because of your kinship to Christ?

_____

_____

_____

_____

_____

_____

~ Pray About It ~

I know there are some things I haven't thanked you for in my life, Lord. I'm sorry for taking these things for granted. Thank you. Thank you for those things I never thanked you for. Thank you for the things you are currently blessing me with... thank you for the work you're doing in me that you haven't finished yet, and thank you most for the Gift only YOU could give, salvation through Jesus your son that promises me You will always be with me no matter where I am in my life's journey. ~ Amen.

Your Team

Day 11
...And The Lord Taketh Away

"But the Israelites did not drive out the people of Geshur and Maakah, so they continue to live among the Israelites to this day" (Joshua 13:13, NLT).

You know the story of the Israelites in the Old Testament of the Bible, right? How they wandered around in the desert for 40 years while they were on the way to the land God had promised them and their descendants? Exodus 23:20-33 tells us about the promises God made to them. They came with strings attached. He said,

> " 'See, I am sending an angel ahead of you to guard you along the way and to bring you to the place I have prepared... My angel will go ahead of you and bring you into the land of the Amorites, Hittites, Perizzites, Canaanites, Hivites and Jebusites, and I will wipe them out. Do not bow down before their gods or worship them or follow their practices. You must demolish them and break their

sacred stones to pieces... Little by little I will drive them out before you, until you have increased enough to take possession of the land. I will establish your borders from the Red Sea to the Sea of the Philistines, and from the desert to the River. I will hand over to you the people who live in the land and you will drive them out before you. Do not make a covenant with them or with their gods. Do not let them live in your land or they will cause you to sin against me, because the worship of their gods will certainly be a snare to you' " (Exodus 23:30-33).

God had clearly promised this land to the Israelites. All they had to do was follow His guidance and the land would be theirs. But they were starting to get tired. Could you imagine traveling like Nomads for 40 years? I get it. My children begged me not to ever move again after our third move in four years. They just wanted to settle, and I understood. After all, I'd moved right along with them! But the Israelites never stopped moving. In Joshua 13:13, the Bible says,

> "But the Israelites did not drive out the people of Geshur and Maakah, so they continue to live among the Israelites to this day."

What does that really mean?

It means God had promised all of Canaan to Israel, but they were tired and they *chose* not to take it.

You see, every bit of everything the Israelites could ever want or need was already given to them—handed to them FROM GOD. All they had to do was take it. God had told them to drive out the people, and their land would belong to Israel, but they chose not to. Every bit of the blessing God had for them was available, but it was more than they were willing to take. **They had what they had because they chose not to take any more.** (We find out later that this does them harm.[3])

Joshua asks them in Joshua 18:3,

> "How long will you wait before you begin to take possession of the land that the Lord, the God of your fathers, has given you?"

Can you ask yourself the same? **What has God already promised you that you just haven't taken possession of?**

Think back along the life of your business. Was there a client you didn't follow up on? A lead who expressed interest at one time in hosting a party, but you never got back with her? Is there someone on your team who is aching for leadership but lacks the self confidence she needs to get started... you noticed, but figured you would just put it on your list of things to do... sometime... later? The idea is, you can have all that you will take. God won't give us more than we're willing to take. Perhaps if your business isn't where you want it to be, it's not because God took it away from you. Perhaps it's because you didn't take what was rightfully yours. He is your business partner! He gave you those leads!

Why would He trust you with more if your (and my!) actions are already telling Him "Thanks Lord, but I have enough?"

The short answer is, **He wouldn't**. If He asks us and we say no, He'll find someone else to do the work, I promise.

I'll tell you, in the beginning of my business, I was terrible at following up. While I felt bad, it was because I was looking at it as lost business or a lost sale, not as a lost opportunity to give that person what GOD wanted them to get from me. Once I started looking at this business as God's business, losing that lead meant that I'd not only taken something He'd given me and given it away to someone else, it meant I'd also just told God "No Thanks, I have plenty." I had regifted God's blessing to someone else! And it was time for that to stop.

~ Think About It ~

What about you? Where in your business have you told God "No thanks, I'm happy where I am. I don't need growth." Take stock of where you fell short. Maybe you did lose that customer to someone who took better care of them. Did you learn anything? Did you ask forgiveness? Maybe you didn't even realize that's what you were doing at the time. Maybe you didn't realize that it wasn't God who took away, but you who told Him you already had enough? Can you see it now?

_____

_____

_____

_____

_____

_____

~ Pray About It ~

Father God, I am so sorry I haven't received the gifts you've given me. I've been lazy, yet labeled it as busy. I've neglected customers, sales, and opportunities you gave me. I haven't used the tools I have available or sought for more to help me accomplish these business tasks. I settled for what I thought was good enough, and where I thought I should be, instead of receiving the gift of where YOU thought I should be. I forgot that this business is our business, and that you would give me strength to take every blessing you have for me. Forgive me for not taking all the "Canaan" you have for me. Give me strength to tackle the tasks I have to do to grow. Give me wisdom and discernment to know what tasks to prioritize, and the contacts I need to take possession of all you have planned for me. In your precious name. ~ Amen.

Day 12
The Grass Is Always Greener In Someone Else's Upline

"At this they wept aloud again. Then Orpah kissed her mother-in-law goodbye, but Ruth clung to her" (Ruth 1:14, NIV).

Do you love your upline? Yes?! Great! Immediately, go call them and tell them how much you love them. Seriously. (They may need a pick me up, and this would certainly do the trick!) For the rest of you, sometimes the skillset that your upline has doesn't mesh with your personality. Or maybe your sponsor quit, and you rolled up to a stranger. Maybe you've never heard from your upline at all, and you resent that she's making money off of you and doesn't even know your name. Or maybe as a founding consultant, your upline is your Home Office, and you have no one to call to lean on.

Sometimes it's hurtful when we do hear about a fellow consultant's wonderful upline, especially if that's an area where we are lacking that leadership and guidance for our own business! We wonder how on earth we got stuck where we are, and why don't we have someone who cares about us as much as Sally's leader cares for her. The grass always seems greener in someone else's upline, doesn't it? But how can we learn to see some green in our own grass? We have to recognize who God places in our life—including Himself—to lead us instead! It could be a fellow consultant, or an upline that isn't even on your team, but somewhere God has someone you can look up to and learn from in the business. You just have to seek them out!

I know a lady who had a lovely wedding and was married and all set to live her happily ever after. She moved across town to where her husband's family lived and was married for ten years when her husband died. In fact, not just her husband, but her brother-in-law, and her father-in-law had also died! Her mother-in-law, Naomi, was devastated. Here she'd lost her husband and two sons in just 10 years! Be it out of love, or out of self pity, Naomi asked her daughters-in-law Ruth and Orpah to leave and go back home to their own families, while she went to her own homeland.

> "May the Lord grant that each of you will find rest in the home of another husband" (Ruth 1:9).

Why should they stay with her, with no chance of remarrying and having a family of their own? They should just go, and she would find some odd job to help make sure she didn't starve.

Orpah said okay, and left for a different upline–a chance to start over with her own family to care for her–maybe even find a man from her own hometown to support her. She left for comfort; it was safer grass, grass she knew once before, grass that would welcome her with open arms. She would ultimately leave Naomi's grass and move back to where the grass of old really did seem greener. But Ruth... Ruth is where God's heart was. You see, Ruth looked up to the woman she respected–her leader, and said,

> "Your people will be my people, and your God, my God" (Ruth 1:16).

Ruth had every reason to leave just as Orpah did, but instead, she chose to trust the person God had chosen as her leader–Naomi. She had no idea how her life would turn out. No idea what the grass looked like if she stayed with Naomi or even if there would be any grass at all, since they had no one to provide for them. No, her situation was not ideal, and yes, she could have had plenty of hurt feelings when Naomi tried to get rid of her. But she listened to the wisdom of her mother-in-law, and allowed this woman of faith to lead her to a place where ultimately, all of her needs would be met by Naomi's God–the very same God we serve today!

Sometimes our situations aren't ideal. We may not see how the upline we have, lineage we have, or even the circumstances we have can possibly lead us. We can feel alone just as Ruth did when her husband died and her mother-in-law asked her to leave. We can be ready to throw in the towel and start over, like Orpah. That's just what Satan would want! Instead, we must recognize who God places in our lives and trust that ultimately, God has a bigger plan than we can imagine! Don't even look at the grass on the other side of the fence, just recognize how God has provided grass right where you are! Seeing your situation, your upline, and downline with the love that God wants us to see them with can help turn even the most challenging upline into a success story just like he did with Ruth and Naomi!

You see, it was Naomi's advice that led Ruth to glean the field (follow along after the harvesters and pick up any leftover grain to bring home and eat) that would be safe for her, rather than risk her safety in the field of strangers. Ruth's character had the townspeople talking about what a good, loyal heart she had. But it was Naomi's wisdom that proved priceless when she advised Ruth to offer herself as a humble servant to the man who would *recognize* her character, and in fact, take her as his wife. It was this man, a godly man, who would provide for both Ruth and Naomi, financially, spiritually, and mentally, as he provided a son for Ruth and a grandson to fill the void Naomi had been missing in her life. And it was the path Ruth stayed on, though the grass may have seemed greener earlier in her life, that would ultimately crown her as the great-grandmother of King David, but more importantly, place her in the lineage of the greatest King there is—Jesus Christ, the King of Kings!

~ Think About It ~

Are there times when you question why God placed you in the upline He did? Are there times when you wish you could be anywhere but where you are? If you look around, can you see a sprig or two of green grass in the field of brown? If you look, is there anywhere you can see a glimmer of hope that can only be God? Look for that fresh blade of green grass right where you are!

~ Pray About It ~

Lord, thank you so much for the vision I know YOU have with this business. Even if I can't see it yet, thank you that YOU have it, and that your word says "I know the plans I have for you, plans for hope and a future, plans to prosper you and not to harm you." Remind me, Lord, when I'm tempted to jump ship or complain about the upline I have, that YOU hand-picked her team the same way you are hand-picking mine. Thank you, Lord for seeing me with the same eyes you saw Ruth and Naomi—full of promise, hope, and a future. ~ Amen

Day 13
When You Feel Like Your Team Hates You

A lady on my team called me and said "My team hates me!"

"Uhhhh... Okay. What do you mean "hates" you?"

"It's like I'm leading and no one is following! And one girl even called the home office and told them I was unsupportive and she wanted a new upline."

She was crushed. Here she was, working to help them and they neither cared nor appreciated her efforts. Once I talked her down off the ledge, we had a talk about some things that she was doing right, and if there was anything she personally felt she needed to work on. We got an action plan together, and everything is now sunshine and unicorns. Through soul searching and prayer, I did my best to help her determine what she needed to work on to help her team be more cohesive.

You know Moses was born as a Hebrew, and the Hebrews were God's people. They were living in Egypt at the time, oppressed as slaves under Egyptian rule. Deep down, the Egyptians were afraid of the Hebrews and their God, and oppression was the way they chose to handle their fear. In fact, the Egyptian Pharaoh had called for every baby Hebrew boy to be killed! Moses' mother had hidden him, and then through miraculous means, given him for adoption to the Pharaoh's daughter to be her son. She had no idea at the time she hid him that he'd be rescued by the daughter of and raised in the very palace of the man who'd ordered his death. In fact, Moses was raised into a fine young man, until one day he made a mistake when he saw an Egyptian beating a Hebrew. Exodus 2:12-14 says,

> "Glancing this way and that, and seeing no one, he killed the Egyptian and hid him in the sand. The next day, he went out and saw two Egyptians fighting. He asked the one in the wrong "Why are you hitting your fellow Hebrew?" The man said "Who made you ruler and judge over us? Are you thinking of killing me as you did the Egyptian?" Then Moses was afraid and thought "What I did must have become known." Then Moses ran from

the Pharaoh, who heard what he did and tried to kill him."

Now you know in Moses' mind, he saw something wrong and tried to "fix it." He saw the Egyptian beating the Hebrew. He thought, *I can right this injustice right now*, and without consulting God, he took matters into his own hands and killed the Egyptian. *Shew!* You know he looked around at that point thinking *"Now what?"* But even the next day, and really, all that time, he was thinking he'd done something to HELP. His Hebrew brothers were on the same team, and he'd just slain their giant! Can I get a whoop whoop around here?!

But instead of treating him with gratitude, his Hebrew "brothers" ratted him out to the Pharaoh, who then tried to kill him! It wasn't that Mo didn't appreciate his upbringing. He just thought Team Mo had more players than just himself. He was wrong. We will never know what might have happened if Moses had waited to respond to the Hebrew beating after inquiring what he should do from God. What we do know is that God's ultimate plan will come, and that with God's help, we can be the leaders he intends for us to be. Later in Moses' life, God specifically asked him to return to Egypt and lead God's people. Moses had every excuse possible for why they wouldn't follow him (after all, they didn't jump on the Team Mo bandwagon the first time, right?).

Exodus 4:10 shows Moses giving excuse after excuse to God.

> "Moses said to The Lord, "O Lord, I have never been eloquent, neither in the past, nor since you have spoken to your servant. I am slow of speech and tongue." The Lord said to him, "Who gave man his mouth? Who makes him deaf or mute? Who gives him sight or makes him go blind? Is it not I, The Lord? Now go, I will help you speak and will teach you what to say."

Action for our teams before (or in the absence of) prayer will never have the outcome we hope. But WITH God leading US to lead *them*, His timing will be perfect and the team we think now hates us will follow us, to follow HIM. Keep on with the task God has for you at hand, knowing that your team is in fact HIS team, and that He has not only hand-picked the people on your team, but chose YOU to be their leader! Believe that He knows what He's doing!

~ Think About It ~

Is your team as close as you'd like? Are you all working as one unit, or does your team dynamic seem like a plate of spaghetti, everyone on their own mission and agenda, in 1,000 different directions? Ask

Him how you can communicate with your team, and what steps He wants you to take with them to be a more cohesive group.

_____

_____

_____

_____

_____

_____

~ Pray About It ~

Lord, I want us all to be on the same page, but sometimes it seems like we aren't even in the same book! I feel like my downline doesn't even want me as their leader! Remind me that you have a purpose for each person on my team, and a reason for having me as their leader! Help me recognize the gifts you have placed in each lady, as well as the best way you want HER to develop those gifts in this business. Help me be a vessel that you can use, and always remind me that because this is YOUR business and your team, You have an ultimate plan that will prosper us, not harm us, and help us as a team bring glory to you! ~ Amen

faith

Day 14
Go Big Or Go Home

"And the Lord said, If you had faith as a grain of mustard seed, you could say unto this sycamine tree, Be plucked up by the root, and be planted in the sea; and it would obey you" (Luke 17:6, KJV, 2000).

I know you've heard that verse before. Someone may have even told you that if you had faith as a grain of mustard seed, you could move mountains! One biblical translation says "If you had faith as small as a grain..." Some take that to mean "You just need a tiny little bit of faith." But wimpy faith won't move mountains, help direct our businesses, OR bring us to a closer relationship with Him! Quite the contrary.

So what is Mustard-Seed-Faith? The Bible says,

"The Kingdom of Heaven is like a grain of mustard seed, which a man took, and sowed in his field; which indeed is smaller than all seeds. But when it is grown, it is greater than the herbs, and becomes a tree, so that the birds of the air come and lodge in its branches" (Matthew 13:31-32).

Mustard-seed-faith isn't small at all! This annual plant–meaning it has to be planted every year–has potential to grow into a 10-12 foot tree from something about the size of the poppy seed on your muffin every year that it's planted! Look at the trees in your yard, or around your workplace. Did they grow 12 feet in a year? Probably not! But if you think about your business–and your faith–don't we all start the same way, as a tiny mustard seed? With our businesses, it's a starter kit and a purposeful desire to grow. With our faith, it's a tiny belief in a God who created us, loved us, and died for us.

That tiny spec of a mustard seed lives out its life continually growing, finishing as a mighty tree! And it does it over and over again, each time it's replanted! So you started small? So what! Don't let your beginning limit your potential! Not in your business, and not in your faith! Not tiny faith. Not mustard-seed-sized faith. What-the-mustard-seed-*becomes* sized-faith! Faith with unlimited potential to do AMAZING things! Not just once, but every planting! Every new catalog, every new campaign!

Sounds easy, right? Just plant and go! But it's not always easy. Sometimes a mustard seed doesn't grow to be 12 feet tall. Those are ideal conditions, after all. We all have ideal planting conditions, and even ideal soil–where we live, and where we plant our business. But that mustard seed will grow in less-than-ideal areas too, and we should too! We won't always have perfect lives, or perfect businesses, or perfect ANYTHING. Keep growing anyway, and bloom where you are planted!

Once you've been planted, then what? God expects consistent, committed character. When jalepenos are planted next to tomatoes, and the seeds from that year's crop are replanted, the tomatoes can taste hot! Characteristics from one plant can leech onto another. However, mustard seeds will always grow to be what God intended them to be! Their commitment is unwavering. God doesn't ever have to be surprised that someone planted mustard and ended up with strawberries!

How awesome would that be if we were that way? Unwavering in our commitment to become what God intends us to become? But we're not always unwavering, are we? We're grumpy when surrounded by naysayers, easily ready to quit when others try to talk us into doing so, disrespectful to our direct selling sisters, or forgetful when it comes to our clients. If that happens, recognize it, squash it, and move on! Just remember your roots, and vow to continue growing!

Jesus told us the birds of the air come to the tree to lodge in its branches. They weren't just coming to look pretty. They were coming to rest their wings. For protection. Comfort. Peace. Shelter. We can be these things for our team, customers, and families!

They came to rest in a tree large enough to support multiple birds. Yes, that tree started small, but faith works miracles with mustard seeds AND with us!

That's the picture God painted for us in Matthew 13. If you are unwavering in your commitment to become a tree, consistent and unaffected by others who try to change you, with a desire to help others, YOU CAN DO ANYTHING. Stop thinking you're still just a seed, when God wants you to move on to the growth phase to be a mighty tree. No more wimpy faith for you! Be greater! Get ready to be unlimited in your faith AND your business, just as God envisions you to be!

~ Think About It ~

Sometimes we are our own worst enemy! Do you still see yourself in the "seed" phase? Are you believing the lie that all you need is to remain the size of the seed, instead of becoming that mighty tree? Or the even bigger lie that you don't have what it takes to *be* 12 feet tall? Squash that!! God wants you to grow! He wants your faith to bloom, to blossom, and to build your family and His kingdom! Staying squashed down like a seed forever means no growth for you, and that's not what God wants! Overcome the doubt that you HAVE THAT POTENTIAL, and go BIG!

_____

_____

_____

More Than Sales

_____

_____

_____

~ Pray About It ~

Thank you, Lord!! I want to be that tree! I want to move beyond thinking that I'm still a seed! Take me and grow me into the woman you would have me be. Unwavering. Unaffected by others. Seeing only your plan. Flexible and willing to do the work to grow to amazing heights in my faith and in this business you've partnered with me! Go with me and guide me as I grow to be EVERYTHING you want me to be!~ AMEN!!

Day 15
When Doubt Creeps In

> "But we had hoped that he was the one who was going to redeem Israel" (Luke 24:21, NIV).

Have you ever heard someone else's voice speak so loudly it drowned out your own? It could be you friend's voice, your kids, your spouse. Eventually, if heard long and loud enough, those voices become the ONLY ones we hear. The same is true for when Satan the enemy speaks. If we listen to him long enough and hard enough, we start to believe the enemy's talk that we aren't where we need to be, in the business we need to be in, or selling what we're selling.

So how do we know which voice to listen to? How can we know for sure that we should be in the direct sales business at all, when it seems like such a struggle at times? Surely God doesn't want His people to struggle with a simple thing such as providing for our families... right?

First, we have to listen to God's voice; the more we listen to it, the more we can recognize Him when He speaks. In John 10:3, the Bible says,

"He calls his own sheep by name and leads them out. When he has brought out all his own, he goes on ahead of them, and his sheep follow him because they know his voice. But they will never follow a stranger; in fact, they will run away from him because they do not recognize a stranger's voice."

You see, the shepherd would come to the gate of the sheep fold and call out for his sheep. Multiple sheep were kept in the same fold at night, guarded by a watchman. When he came for them, the sheep would follow their shepherd to new pastures with green grass and rivers of water to drink. He would talk to them, guide them, keep them in line, rescue them, and defend them. If they were in trouble, he was there. If they needed rest, he was there to carry them. He knew the mannerisms of each sheep, because he spent his time caring for and about them.

But how much more are we loved than sheep? We are the only one of God's creations that are made in His image. He cries over us, sings over us (Zephaniah 3:17), rejoices over us, and grieves over us (Luke 19:41). Yet routinely, we doubt that the voice we heard was God's. Or we hear it and seem so sure of it at the time, and then something comes along to deter us from our path.

What's a girl to do?

First, take heart. Even Jesus' very own disciples doubted at times. Right after Jesus was crucified, his followers–disciples included–were distraught. Here they had told everyone that He was the Messiah; the one who was going to save Israel from oppression and Roman rule. Luke 24:15-21 says,

> "As they talked and discussed these things with each other, Jesus himself came up and walked along with them; but they were kept from recognizing him.
>
> He asked them, "What are you discussing together as you walk along?"
>
> They stood still, their faces downcast. One of them, named Cleopas asked him, "Are you the only one visiting Jerusalem who does not know the things that have happened there in these days?"
>
> "What things?" he asked.
>
> "About Jesus of Nazareth," they replied. "He was a prophet, powerful in word and deed before God and all the people. The chief priests and our rulers handed him over to be sentenced to death, and they crucified him; but we had hoped

that he was the one who was going to redeem Israel."

Here were two of Jesus' own disciples who didn't recognize Him, and they walked with Him every day! If THEY couldn't recognize Him, how can we have any hope at all?

We have to be like sheep, who listen to their shepherd! We have to be like the sheep that run away from a stranger's call, running toward the one who knows us, loves us, and created us! He didn't just create you en masse. He knit you together in your mother's womb. To knit is to piece together, stitch by stitch, loop by loop, thread by thread. He knows your inner workings, and knows, just like that shepherd does, when you are weak and need to hear His voice to call you back!

How do you get back? Seek out your shepherd. Don't be like the disciples who weren't sure where to turn next. Because just as we are to know His voice, he knows our voice as well, and will come running to rescue us, answer us, and comfort us. Satan can't ever take away our salvation or our shepherd. But He can confuse us, mimic God's voice, and make us ineffective so that we stop in our tracks, rather than take any steps at all.

~ Think About It ~

Are you at a crossroads? It may be in business, or in a decision with your kids, your family, or even your friends. Are you finding it hard to discern which voice is God's amongst all the others? Worse yet, ready to walk away from all the voices, sit in the corner and have a good cry? What affirmative answer do you need from your Shepherd to eliminate your doubts and help you find your way back to Him?

_____

_____

_____

_____

_____

_____

~ Pray About It ~

Father God, I know You are my Shepherd, but sometimes it's so hard to hear You in the noise. There are so many voices, and I can't tell which is you. Sometimes none of them sound like you, and sometimes ALL of them do. Please Lord, lead me beside the still waters. Restore my soul. I know you are my Shepherd, and this is your sheep calling out to you to rescue me and lead me where you want me to go. Erase my doubt, help me hear you, and make my next step clear. In Your precious name. ~Amen.

Day 16
I CAN'T

"When they saw the courage of Peter and John and realized they were unschooled, they were astonished and took note that these men had been with Jesus" (Acts 4:13, NIV).

You've heard that old cliche "God doesn't call the qualified, he qualifies the called." Essentially , it means that God doesn't use only those who are talented, or Upper Level Double Diamonds, Senior Executive Directors, or Elite Directors. He uses anyone He wants to further His kingdom and ANYONE–including you can be qualified to do ! I know what you're thinking: BUT I CAN'T. Can't sell, can't teach, can't walk up and talk to people. I don't have a degree in marketing, or 10 years of sales experience. I'm just a (insert word here, mom, wife, person in the city, person in the country, etc).

First, God doesn't make "justas." He makes every single person unique, with a unique gift or talent or contribution that they bring to the world. There is no such thing as just a mom. Or just a video game player. Or just a woman who has three cats and loves chocolate. There simply are no justas.

Knowing that you were created for a purpose and every single thing about you is special, how do you know you can't? I was in a coaching session once where we replaced the one word can't with two words in its place. HAVEN'T YET.[4] Instead of "I can't teach," it's "I haven't yet taught... but I can do anything through Christ who strengthens me."

Instead of "I can't sell," it's "I haven't yet sold much, but I can do anything through Christ who strengthens me!" I make it sound too easy, don't I? But it's not me who gives you the strength, it's God; the same way that He did for Peter and John.

Peter and John were talking to a group of people after Jesus' death. The day before, they had healed a man who had been lame his entire life, simply by speaking it in Jesus' name. The people were amazed, but Peter and John could take no credit for it. Peter said to them,

> " "People of Israel," he said, "what is so surprising about this? And why stare at us as though we had made this man walk by our own power or godliness? For it is the God of Abraham, Isaac, and Jacob — the God of all our ancestors — who has brought glory to his servant Jesus by doing this. This is the same Jesus whom you handed over and rejected before Pilate, despite Pilate's decision to release him. You rejected this holy, righteous

one and instead demanded the release of a murderer. You killed the author of life, but God raised him from the dead. And we are witnesses of this fact!

"Through faith in the name of Jesus, this man was healed—and you know how crippled he was before. Faith in Jesus' name has healed him before your very eyes.

"Friends, I realize that what you and your leaders did to Jesus was done in ignorance. But God was fulfilling what all the prophets had foretold about the Messiah—that he must suffer these things. Now repent of your sins and turn to God, so that your sins may be wiped away" " (Acts 3:12-19, NLT).

They acknowledged that yes, the people had done wrong in condemning Jesus, but it had to be done to fulfill prophecy!

While Peter and John were speaking to the people, they were confronted by the priests, the captain of the Temple guard, and some of the Sadducees, who were, shall we say, freaking out a bit. They arrested Peter and John for teaching the people, but even more people–about 5,000–had come to believe. The next morning, the high priest was there to try them for healing the man, and for speaking about Jesus.

"Annas the high priest was there, along with Caiaphas, John, Alexander, and other relatives of the high priest. They brought in the two disciples and demanded, "By what power, or in whose name, have you done this?"

Then Peter, filled with the Holy Spirit, said to them, "Rulers and elders of our people, are we being questioned today because we've done a good deed for a crippled man? Do you want to know how he was healed? Let me clearly state to all of you and to all the people of Israel that he was healed by the powerful name of Jesus Christ the Nazarene, the man you crucified but whom God raised from the dead. For Jesus is the one referred to in the Scriptures, where it says, 'The stone that you builders rejected has now become the cornerstone" (Acts 4:6-11, NLT).

Now here's the kicker; the council members? They could see Peter and John, that they were unschooled, ordinary men with no special training. But they knew that despite that, the stamp on their very being was so clearly marked "disciple of Jesus"

More Than Sales

that even without Jesus being present, He was present in them.

And look what they had done! They healed people, in Jesus' name! They led 5,000 people in one sitting to Christ!

Yet here we are, with our packet of catalogs, and our telephone in hand saying "I can't." YES YOU CAN! These men were ordinary. They were "Justas" without Jesus, but limitless with Jesus. That very same Jesus that was present in them? He's in *you*, if you're His child.

You have the same unlimited God that they had. You don't have to raise dead, heal lame, or bring 5,000 to God. But with his help, you can sell, you can teach, you can lead, and you can provide for yourself and your family, not because of who you are, but because of WHOSE you are.

~ Think About It ~

Have you been limiting God? Have you said "I can't" or "I'm just" when God is waiting for you to realize the power you have in Him, especially with Him as your business partner? What one thing have you said "I can't" or "I'm just" to? Is there an "I can't" that could change your whole business if you saw it through the unlimited eyes of God? What one "I can't" can you replace with "I haven't yet", and then, replace with "I DID!"?

_____

_____

_____

_____

_____

_____

~ Pray About It ~

Father God, I can't. But you can! Help me see that I'm not Justa. Help me see that I CAN do it! Help me go from Justa to Peter and John in front of the council. I want to be the woman that others can look at and see you, see your stamp on me, see me as capable of holding my own with the highest of the high, just as Peter and John were. Remind me that where I can't, you can. Help me see myself the way you do, not pridefully so, but empowered and enabled through you. In your name. ~Amen.

Personal Growth

Day 17
REJECTION

So you finally got the nerve to go beyond your initial circle of friends to start offering the party opportunity to strangers. Woo hooo! You've got your list of leads and prospects, and start calling or texting.

"Hi, it's Sally, your Favorite Personal Jeweler. We have a super awesome special this month on your favorite bracelet and I remembered you liked that bracelet. I only have a few more hostess slots open. What day of the week works best to have a party?"

You ask a similar question to ten others. You get eight people who don't respond at all, one who says she's moving, and one who harshly says "No thanks."

Ugh.

That one who says "no thanks"... it cuts like a knife doesn't it? It's like they literally rip out your heart from your chest and throw it back at you! How on earth are you supposed to send your kids to college / pay the bills / get out of debt / buy a new house, etc etc if nine people in a row say no?

It's enough to hang it all up and go work nights at a pizza joint.

Rejection is hard. It's hard when someone rejects your party offer, and it's hard when someone unsubscribes from your monthly newsletter. Or at least it is for me. Your upline will encourage you and say "They just don't know a good thing when they see it." But truthfully, each rejection tears away a little bit of your exterior until all you have left is open and exposed… and wounded. Rejection dashes your hopes and squashes your dreams, with each "no," "not now," and "unsubscribe."

There was someone else who felt rejection – someone else who was left literally hanging out to dry. Joseph was one of 12 brothers. Sure he was a bit cocky, knowing he was his dad's favorite of all the brothers. But that one afternoon when Joseph went to visit his brothers in the field at his dad's request, they were so sick and tired of him they threw him in a well! And of course they couldn't kill him so they did the next best thing–they sold him off to a roving caravan as a slave. (Granted, a simple "no thanks" seems a lot less life-threatening now, doesn't it?)

Can you imagine his thoughts as he's being hitched to the slave ropes and cattle-driven away?

"Uh guys? Hey guys? This isn't funny anymore!"

Lonely, abandoned, afraid, and rejected at 17, Joseph was immediately plunged into a new world where there was no escape. But even though he was rejected by his brothers and sold off to slavery, he still had the hand of God on him. He was purchased by Pharaoh's Captain of the Guard, Potiphar. Genesis 39 :2-4 says,

> "The Lord was with Joseph so that he prospered, and he lived in the house of his Egyptian master. When his master saw that the Lord was with him and that the Lord gave him success in everything he did, Joseph found favor in his eyes and became his attendant. Potiphar put him in charge of his household, and he entrusted to his care everything he owned."

Joseph worked hard, and was a man of good character. So much so that even when Mrs. Potiphar tried to seduce Joseph, he denied her advances and rejected her. Listen to what he said: "How can I leave God who has given me so much, to do this bad thing?" He saw, even as a slave, even after rejection from his family, that God was always by his side. Mrs. Potiphar would have none of that, and her character was not strong or full of faith. She accused Joseph of rape, and had him thrown into prison.

Joseph just can't catch a break. Do you ever feel like that? Like even if you ARE doing the right thing, it still ends up not in your favor?

While in prison, Joseph continued to work hard, and he continued to have God's favor on him, earning quite the reputation as a man of God. Everyone could see God's hand on Joseph.

> "But while Joseph was there in the prison, the Lord was with him; he showed him kindness and granted him favor in the eyes of the prison warden. So the warden put Joseph in charge of all those held in the prison, and he was made responsible for all that was done there. The warden paid no attention to anything under Joseph's care, because the Lord was with Joseph and gave him success in whatever he did" (Genesis 39:21-23).

And, he was able to do something no one else in the entire kingdom could do—use his God-given wisdom to interpret two troubling dreams the Pharaoh had had. The Pharaoh could see that no one else in his kingdom had the wisdom and abilities that Joseph had. Joseph was not just released from prison, but was given a high place of honor in the kingdom because of his character, his integrity, and his favor with God. Here's a person who had been rejected by everyone he loved, except God. But no matter what adverse conditions he was introduced to, he overcame them with God's help.

~ Think About It ~

Here's the thing. Yes, rejection does hurt, but it's God's plan for you to pick yourself up and keep going. The same God that made a miracle out of Joseph's rejection wants to do the same for you, if you'll let Him. Yes, you might be unsubscribed. Yes, you'll have people come right out and say "no thanks," while others say nothing at all. Yes, you'll have people tell you you're crazy, and want nothing to do with your product – even your own family members!

Your only task is to make God's voice louder than the rest.

Can you bring your broken, rejected, defeated, and hurting self to Jesus, and block out the noise and rejection from the rest of the world to hear His voice? His voice says "You can do this." His voice says "I will provide for you." His voice says "You are worthy of every good thing in my kingdom." His voice says "Fear not." His voice whispers "Come to me, all who are weary and burdened and I will give you rest" and it shouts from the mountaintop "If God is for you, who can be against you?"

Are you ready to believe that God has more for you if you'll be as Joseph, strong in character and rock-solid in faith, regardless of rejection from others? Can you make God's voice louder than those who have rejected you? Which voice have you let become louder than God's? Are you ready to reverse those roles and let God's voice boom over the rest?

_____

_____

_____

_____

_____

_____

~ Pray About It ~

Dear Lord, this rejection hurts, and I'm so over it! I want to believe that YOU have more for me, and that if I keep trying and stay the course, that you will provide more than I can ever imagine, but those outside voices are so loud. Help me place mufflers on my ears that block out those voices and hear only yours; yours that tells me I am loved, I am provided for, and I am worthy of the things you have waiting for me. I trust you to replace those who have not partnered in our business with new customers. I claim victory over the defeat of rejection! I thank you for all you are doing to not just prosper this business, but to help me become the woman you desire me to be, and bring me closer to you. ~ Amen

Day 18
Thou Shalt Not Covet Thy Neighbor's Business

"Is anything too hard for the Lord? I will return to you at the appointed time next year and Sarah will have a son" (Genesis 18:14, NIV).

"And the top in sales this month goes toooooooo…. Sally Seller! Wooo hooo"

You clap for her, but your inner mean girl is squinting your eyes and muttering under your breath about what trick she must have used, or how she had an unfair advantage because you worked three weekends in a row at your second job and couldn't party as much as she did. *What's her secret? Surely she has something special on her side that I don't have.*

Month after month you see Sally, then Betty, then Wanda, get all the glory, while your name moves further and further down the list of has-been consultants. The next month, you try everything up your sleeve to get parties and sales, all the while Sally struts off, taking another "top seller" prize.

Maybe it's not top in sales, maybe you signed up before she did, and she promoted first. Maybe you've NEVER promoted, but should have and can't figure out why. Maybe another entire team does better than yours. Your prayers, while earnest, sound a bit like this: "But why God? How come she has half the team members that I do with double the sales? It's not fair! I don't get it! Will you make me like Sally, Lord? Please?" And maybe you cry, real tears, because you just can't see why God won't give you what He's given her. You promise God this or that, if only He would make your business booming like Sally's.

I know someone who's been in your shoes. (I mean besides me, and probably every other consultant who's ever signed up for any company, *ever*.) Sarai. Sarai was married to Abram, who was very close to God. In Bible times, children were considered not just a heritage from the Lord, but a blessing. The more children you had, the more blessed you were. A woman who could not give her husband a child was considered "USELESS."

Sarai and Abram had been together for many years, but she had never been pregnant. Though beautiful, Sarai was barren, and this was cause for divorce in those times. She wept and wept, asking God "Why? Why do these other women have babies, and I have nothing to give my husband?" She blamed God for making the other women fruitful, and for making her fruitless. Abram, a man who trusted God with every fiber of his being, and had left his home country to follow God, told her not to worry.

God told them he would be a father to not just one child, but to as many as stars were in the sky! Abram had followed God faithfully, and God had promised him,

> "To your offspring, I will give this land." (Genesis 12:7)

But even he began to lose faith in God's promise. Genesis 15:2 says,

> "But Abram said, 'O Sovereign Lord, since I remain childless, and the one who will inherit my estate is Eliezer of Damascus?' "

Eliezer was Abram's head servant, and without a blood heir, Abram would have left everything to him. It just wasn't fair. Everywhere around him, OTHER families were living on the land God had promised him! So how was it that he was going to ever see either the promise of offspring *or* land?

So here's Sarai, looking around at her old, wrinkly, 90-year old body thinking "This guy has lost his mind! I can't give him thousands of children! I can't even give him ONE." And Sarai's heart was broken. The communal method of living back then meant that she had to be around other children from the village that belonged to other moms. Weekly.

Daily. Hourly. Sarai saw the blessings that were bestowed on other women and she coveted the same thing for herself, with no solution in sight.

Until the day Sarai hatched a plan.

"Hmmm, so Abram is meant to be a father to many. Maybe I'll have him sleep with my servant, and they'll have a son, and that'll be almost the same as if he had one with me." At the time, servants and nursemaids were property, so if Sarai's nursemaid was to lay with Abram, it was an extension of her own self. Sarah arranges a night's stay between her servant Hagar and Abram. Of course, badaboom, badabing, Hagar conceives, and nine months later, Abraham DOES become a father. But Sarai's heart was even more jealous than it was before, and Hagar despises the situation she's been put in, as well as Sarai herself!

Now, the covetousness she'd felt in her heart for other children outside of her family was replaced with envy and bitterness. Envy over her nursemaid's child with her husband, and bitterness... because the proof was there that all along it was *her* inadequacies that could not provide for Abram. Abram and Sarai felt lost and hopeless even when God himself came to tell Abram of his promises.

God changed Abram's name to Abraham, which meant "Father of many" and changed Sarai's name to Sarah. Abram *laughed at God*. "Will a son be born to a man a hundred years old? Will Sarah bear a child at the age of ninety?" But God did not give up on Abraham, OR Sarah, despite their doubt. Sarah

More Than Sales

even laughs at the Lord! God asks her "Is anything too hard for the Lord?" She lied and said she hadn't laughed, but He knew she had, and He called her out on the carpet for her lack of faith.

God had intended to provide for Abraham and Sarah all along. It was Sarah's lack of faith in God's provision that made her take matters into her own hands with Hagar. Yes, she'd heard what Abraham said about being a father to many nations, but she truly didn't believe that God could do it through her, even when God himself had said it! God did work through her, even in her doubt, just as He does with us. Sarah had wanted God to give her many, many children throughout her life, but the ONE he did give her was worth all of them.

~ Think About It ~

What about you? Do you truly believe that God's plans for you are better than your own? Do you have faith that God wants the business you're in together to thrive or are you working your business in fear, doubtful of God's provision? Are you afraid that this month is going to be just like the rest, a nail-biter til the very end? Are you doubting your own business skills and the plans God has for you to transform your life and your relationship with Him?

Are you Sarai, doubting and taking matters into your own hands, or will you be Sarah, transformed by faith into a woman God has unlimited favor for?

~ Pray About It ~

Please forgive me. I've doubted your provision. I've replaced happiness for my business friend with jealousy, envy, and bitterness. I just didn't see where you had enough love and provision for both of us. Help me to see that you have untold treasures I haven't even thought of, just waiting for me to grasp them, if only I would trust that you have them for me. Help me remember that you are the very same powerful God that you were with Sarah. Mend the relationship with my colleague so I can look at her with love, not with eyes of selfishness. Make this business all that YOU want it to be, not all that I want it to be. In your name, Amen.

Day 19
Comparison Is The Thief Of Joy[5]

"(Speaking about Jesus Christ) Who, being in very nature God, did not consider equality with God something to be used to his own advantage; rather, he made himself nothing by taking the very nature of a servant, being made in human likeness" (Philippians 2:6, NIV).

Sometimes we compare ourselves to others and covet their business. Other times... our disappointment lies only in ourselves. We set a goal to be a certain level; Director, Diamond, Senior Executive; and when that doesn't happen, it's easy to think we have failed... even if our business as a whole is successful.

It's easy to get discouraged and think that because we didn't get there *yet*, we never will. I know leaders that hit one of the first levels of leadership very quickly, then stayed there for *years*. They had high personal sales! High team sales! But took years to make it to that second level of promotion. Some of them *still* haven't made it, and they search themselves every day wondering what they're doing wrong, and why they don't have what it takes to be the next level leader. Listen, God doesn't want you to live feeling defeated! On the contrary!

When Paul wrote to the church in Philippi, he was writing from prison. Not prison for murdering someone, or theft, but prison for being a disciple. He wrote to encourage the Philippians, and told them his greatest joy would simply be for them to be like-minded, of one spirit and mind. When he said this, he didn't mean they all needed to think like *each other*, rather, they needed to all think *like Christ!*

His charge to them was simple: Do nothing out of selfish ambition or vain conceit (vs 3). Rather, value others above yourselves, not looking to your own interests, but looking to the interests of others! That's the same thing we need to be reminded of with our teams; it's not about promoting them to get our own title bumped up. It's about helping them develop as a leader and as a woman, in God's time, not ours. And then he (Paul) reminded them of something critical. He said,

> "have the same mindset as Jesus! Who, being by his very nature God, never used his equality with God to his advantage!"

You'd think he would, right? "Look at my TITLE! I'm JESUS!" No, he never did—not once. When Jesus spoke about His Father, it was reverent, and full of love and honor. He never talked about God in a way that people felt He was beyond their reach! Paul goes on to tell us that instead of being prideful and reminding us who he was, Jesus took on the nature of a servant, humbling himself, and dying on a cross for a humanity that didn't deserve it then, and doesn't deserve it now! For his reward, Jesus was exalted, and given a name that is higher than any other name!

Did you read that, or did you just skim? I'll repeat it. Jesus never used his equality with God–his title or his status–to do the work He was sent here to do. *His* title didn't matter to him! Only the title of His Father, and the task God had given Him mattered.

When Jesus followed in obedience to God, His reward was far greater than anything humans could imagine. God exalted him, gave him a name above every other, a name at which every knee bows, both in heaven and on earth, and a name which every tongue confesses that he is Lord!

So what does that have to do with us? And comparing ourselves with the "us" that we think we should be? Everything! You see God worked in His Son Jesus, to fulfill his good purpose (vs 13). If God rewards His Son for obedience, and for putting aside vanity and his "title and stature" in the heavens so that he could come down to earth, humble himself, and do the work that God had for him, wouldn't he reward *us* for doing the same? Granted, we didn't descend from heaven, but we will be rewarded for our obedience, and for putting aside our vanity, titles and statures!

I'm not saying don't work for goals and titles–I LOVE goals–both making them and meeting them, and yes I love new promotion titles too! But God is not concerned with your title–only that you do the work He has tasked for you with your team–sharing His love, nurturing their hearts, and being their mentor to move them forward in their business. When we do that we honor HIM, and the rewards He has for us will come with the level of awesomeness that only God has. Comparing yourself to even what YOU think you should be or a level or title you think you should have undermines the true tasks and goals that God has for your business.

~ Think About It ~

The enemy Satan is the one that whispers in your ear that you aren't enough, that you should give up, and that if you haven't promoted yet, you never will. But you see, that's not his call to make! It's God's! And as long as you are doing the work that God has for you, His rewards are much greater than anything we can imagine. Don't be discouraged about what Satan wants you to believe concerning your title. Instead, be encouraged by what God's word TELLS YOU. Look to your team and their interests, and God will work out the details of your rewards!

Titles and levels all fall away at the foot of the cross. Let your focus be on aligning your business with God's, and the promotions, titles, and rewards will come as we honor and glorify Him!

Is there someone is your business that you find yourself constantly comparing yourself with? That's not what God wants for you! Is there personal disappointment in not meeting your own plan for your business? What areas do you need to give to God so He can show you his goals and rewards for you?

_____

_____

_____

_____

_____

_____

~ Pray About It ~

Lord, it is so discouraging when I haven't met my own goals. I doubt myself, my goals, my place in this business, and my leadership abilities. Sometimes I want to throw in the towel altogether.

But Lord, forgive me. I have taken my eyes off of YOUR goals for this business, and placed them on superficial titles and rewards. Please send me a reminder of why I'm here, and help me see that my long-term business goals are to glorify you in our business venture. Remind me that your rewards come in perfect timing, and that you are not slow as we understand slow. Thank you, Lord for having your hand ever on this business. In your name, Amen.

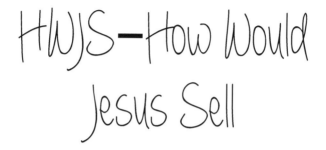

HWJS—How Would
Jesus Sell

Day 20
When You've Made A Mistake

"Now go and tell his disciples, including Peter, that Jesus is going ahead of you to Galilee. You will see him there, just as he told you before he died" (Mark 16:7, NLT).

You know it. That feeling you get in the pit of your stomach when you've screwed up. Like someone sucker punched you. It knocks the wind out of your sails and your feet out from under you. Sometimes, it's because of something you did. Maybe you got caught in a lie to a customer, or you did something mean to another consultant to sabotage her business and improve your own. Maybe it wasn't intentional, but as soon as it happened, you knew what that familiar feeling was.

Probably one of the worst screw-ups I've ever made in my business was with another gal who was hosting a Christmas get-together with several other vendors. We were to meet at her house, and there were four of us. I signed up to come, and bring a table of my products but didn't follow through. When people started saying they would be late, I took that as permission for me to be late too. I didn't realize they'd all made agreements, and I was giving myself permission to back out of my commitment. When it came time for the event, which I'd been invited to as a GUEST vendor from one of the main vendors to begin with, I told myself my presence didn't matter at all, and opted out completely.

I was wrong. My presence *did* matter.

They needed me, and I'd let them down.   I blamed everybody but myself, and sadly, burned that bridge as well as the bridges with the other vendors. That event was years ago, but it still haunts me, because I gave myself permission to screw up, and handed those business connections over to another consultant who would undoubtedly not blow off Christmas gatherings at another gracious representative's home.

We all make mistakes, not thinking of the consequences at the time, thinking it won't hurt anyone.

Peter sure did. He was Jesus' disciple, and one of the original four. He was devoted to Jesus, and loved him more than a brother. When Jesus knew the time for His ultimate sacrifice was near, He told Peter that before the rooster crowed, Peter would deny Jesus not once, not twice, but three times. Of course Peter didn't believe him. They were buds. Jesus was his leader, his teacher, and Peter had given up

More Than Sales

everything to follow Jesus as a disciple. But that night, as Jesus was being led away to be crucified, Peter did deny knowing Jesus. Not once. Not twice. Three times. Can you imagine the feeling in the pit of Peter's stomach when he heard the rooster crow? He should have stood up for Jesus!

Why was he afraid? He would never have a chance to make that screw up right. Jesus had died and Peter was heartbroken. This man of miracles, of healing, grace, and mercy was crucified and tortured on a cross. Peter would never have the chance to say he was sorry. They buried Jesus' body in a tomb, rolled a boulder in front of it and armed it with guards so no one would steal the body. But even death couldn't conquer Jesus, and he rose from the dead 3 days later. Angels rolled the boulder away so Jesus could come out, and do you know one of the first things he said?

"Go tell my disciples and Peter."

That doesn't even make sense; Peter WAS a disciple. Why would Jesus single him out? Had Jesus disowned Peter because of his actions? Had Peter been booted from the discipleship, banished from Jerusalem forever?

No. It's because He knew Peter would not have forgiven himself. He knew that Peter would blame himself, his soul burdened with the guilt he felt over denying Jesus. But Jesus wanted Peter, specifically, to know that He held no blame on him. He needed Peter to know that he was not a screw up, and no matter what Peter thought or believed about himself, Jesus still loved him.

It's the same with us. Yes, we can burn a customer bridge. Yes, we can screw up and say something ugly to another consultant, or even exhibit unChristlike behavior. But it's all capable of being laid at the feet of Jesus in forgiveness. The Bible says in 1 John 1:9 that,

> "If we confess our sins, He is faithful and just to forgive them, and to cleanse us from all the wrongs we have done."

Just like Peter, God will take whatever mistakes you've made with this business you own with Him, forgive them, and then move on. He didn't harbor anger or hold a grudge with Peter, and He won't with you.

~ Think About It ~

Is there somewhere in your business you feel incredible guilt? A past mistake that you still feel judgment for, or a current issue you just can't get past? Do you believe that God can forgive you for anything, pick you up, dust you off, and set you back on the right path? He will!

_____

_____

_____

_____

_____

_____

~ Pray About It ~

Father God, I still can't believe I did that. What was I thinking? I screwed up this whole business with one major mistake–this business YOU gave me to take care of, and what did I do? I screwed it up! And I'm afraid I'll do it again! Father God, please forgive me. Forgive me for the mistakes I've made in both my business and in my personal life. I want to be like Peter, where you single me out and tell me directly of your forgiveness. Remind me when I try to bring it back up next week or next month that you've not only forgiven it, but you've forgotten it. Give me wisdom to recognize the temptation to do it again, and guide my paths to stay the course that you have set for me. In your name, Amen.

Day 21
Enough Business For Everyone: Saturation

"What causes fights and quarrels among you? Don't they come from your desires that battle within you? You desire but do not have, so you kill. You covet but you cannot get what you want, so you quarrel and fight. You do not have because you do not ask God. When you ask, you do not receive, because you ask with wrong motives, that you may spend what you get on your pleasures" (James 4:1-3, NIV).

Saturation can apply EVERYWHERE. Don't believe me? Look in the phone book. How many doctors do you see? Probably a big section. Lawyers? McDonalds'? How many Smiths? How many Joneses?

And someone (yes, I have naysayers too) will ask why I'm spending time writing devotions when you can find devotions by much more popular authors on the shelves. Matter of fact, how many devotionals are there out there, period? The answer to all of the above is the same: A LOT!

You might be feeling like there are a lot of consultants or representatives in your area; there very may well be! So why should you continue? Everybody knows a consultant! And if not you, invariably someone on your team will come to you with the same claim, and need your listening ear. She'll say, "My area is completely saturated, and sales are impossible!"

It may seem that way—or at least that's what we tell ourselves!

Do you remember back on Day 1 of this book, when you thought about your kit, and I told you that you had God in your box along with your products? And do you remember when we asked God to be our CEO? Now let me ask you this: Can God fail? *"No, but I can,"* you say.

It's so easy to give up, or look around and see every single person carrying or wearing your product and you *know* they didn't get it from you. It can cause jealousy, bitterness, and a loss of hope. I know, I live in a small town and just within a 20 minute radius, we have nearly 20 leadership-level women painting the town with all of our products—that's not even including their teams. That number is just *leaders.* So I know what it's like. I know that feeling of excitement when you go up to tell a person about your product and she looks at you with her lip curled and says "Oh I already have a friend who sells this," or "My cousin sells," or "I just did a party."

But that's just what Satan would want you to do, and let's be honest, that's what your competitors want you to do as well. If you throw in the towel, where will your customers go? To them, of course! But let's find out what God's Word says about saturation. First, the disciple and writer Paul put it best in reminding us,

"If God is for us, who can be against us?"

That alone should be sufficient to tell you that GOD, your CEO, has nothing that can stop Him. Not even the dreaded s-word. It's worth repeating:"If God is for us, who can be against us?" Why is it so easy for us to forget that? Fear. Desperation. Tiredness. *Oh, I don't know, everything else going wrong in life?* You know, not even being able to go to the bathroom by yourself without someone following you in dire need of SOMETHING, medical conditions, or even a situation where you HAVE to be the breadwinner, because there's no one else who can.... just everyday life makes us tired! Any number of things can take our eyes off of our mission, our business, our God, and make us put them where they shouldn't be—watching everyone else's business flourishing. The disciple James said in James 4,

> "What causes fights and quarrels among you? Don't they come from your desires that battle within you? You desire but

More Than Sales

do not have, so you kill. You covet but you cannot get what you want, so you quarrel and fight. You do not have because you do not ask God. When you ask, you do not receive, because you ask with wrong motives, that you may spend what you get on your pleasures."

Let me tell you a funny story about my daughter. About once a week, she would ask us for a kitten. She loves cats, and wanted one of her very own. Now, we have two dogs already, and her daddy had already laid down the law: 2 pets maximum at a time.

"But why daddy?" she'd ask. "Why can't I have a kitty?"

"Two pets at a time, max. No new animals until one of the ones we have passes."

A week later, it was deja vu, with the same series of questions. About 6 months ago, she started showing him pictures of the cat she would get. She started selecting shirts with little cats on them as her new outfits for school. She told her daddy what she would name her cat when he got it for her (not if, but when). One day, after we had just bought a new house, they drove past a kitten who'd been run over. Something in her daddy's heart had melted over all this time, and he went back to rescue it, but it was too late, the kitten had died by the time he could turn around.

My daughter however, asked even more questions about homeless kitties who had no family to love them and keep them safe from passing cars. She promised her next cat (so sure of herself, and that God would provide) would be from a shelter. Daily she reminded us of how much she wanted one. What's my point? Just this: Twitchy Bigglesworth, a sweet 5-lb, 1-yr old cat was rescued from the animal shelter last weekend, and guess where she lives? In. Our. House. WITH the two dogs. And her daddy.

You see, my daughter doesn't know anything about saturation. It's not in her vocabulary, not because she doesn't use big words, but because her faith that she *could* was bigger than the voices telling her she couldn't. She doesn't know how many cats live in this area, how many are homeless, and how many have homes. She just knew that she wanted one. She would ask me "But mommy, why can't we just have that stray kitty and give him a home?" And I would say "Because we want a kitty that wants to be our kitty. We want one that will be loyal and love our family so much she would never leave to go be with another family like s stray cat would." Somewhere out there was the perfect kitty who was waiting to come home with us, even though it may not have known it yet. In her prayers, this 7 yr old relentlessly asked God, and her parents for the thing she wanted most. And you know what? She got it! She traded in the toys she would have gotten for her birthday for a litter box and cat perch, and brought home a very sweet, snuggly, spoiled rotten ball of fur.

James tells us to ask, and keep on asking. Let's say you pray one time and ask God to show you how to get started after a slump, or ask for new business after a move. Whose prayer do you think He'll answer? The one who asks once or twice, not even sure of what they want? Or the one who asks daily...weekly...hourly, in humbleness "Lord, please show me a way to provide for my family. Please show me where to find this hostess. Please give me strength to ask someone new."

I knew right away that when we were driving home from the shelter with our meowing box that God was speaking to my own heart about saturation. *Do you see?* He asked. *This girl knew what she wanted and asked for it. She was swayed by nothing. She prayed for it, knowing I could provide somehow. A one-time prayer for something doesn't show Me you desire something; be relentless.* Saturation is no match for God. If you want to succeed, and you're sure, be relentless about asking God to help your business prosper. Show Him all the things you'll do with your money. Take actions as if you do believe! Be a good steward with the money you have, proving to Him that you can take on more, and don't stop asking until God answers your prayer. Be relentless in your pursuit of the dreams and the plans God has for you.

~ Think About It ~

There will always be someone who can do what you're doing. Always someone selling what you have. But do you think that God is bigger than your "saturated" market? If so, then we need to have a talk about whether or not you truly believe God's omnipotence exceeds the reach of your business. It's not about whether He cares if your business succeeds. Of course He does. But do you? Have you given up? Have you stopped asking God to provide? Or have you succumbed to Satan's whispers that you need to move on? Don't give him that satisfaction! Where in your business can you be relentless to ask God to help remove those thoughts of saturation, and replace them with thoughts of sufficiency, abundance, and provision?

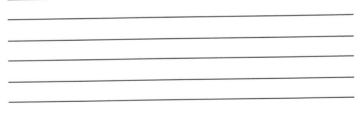

~ Pray About It ~

Dear Lord, I've given up. There are so many people in sales, and so many people who have somebody already. I need You to help me restart and grow this business. I don't want just new customers, Lord. I want to be the kind of consultant that You want

More Than Sales

representing YOU as YOUR business partner. I want You to proudly bring people to me and whisper to them, "Work with Karen, she's My business partner." Lord, I ask you to bring customers to me, but also show me how to bring them in myself. I will take action Lord, because I believe you are already providing and making a way for me. ~Amen

Day 22
Loving The Unlovables:
Negative Nancys

"They said, "Is this not Jesus, the son of Joseph, whose father and mother we know? How can he now say, 'I came down from heaven'?" "Stop grumbling among yourselves," Jesus answered" (John 6:42, 43, NIV).

You know you have those women in your business. They may be in your upline, probably are in your downline, may be your neighbors, and even in your customer pool. There's always something they don't like. Your product is made in China, or the shipping is too high, or why can't they see it online, or have to see it only at a Boutique... it's always something with them. Something they can earn for free isn't the thing they wanted for free, the 4-person circle of friends they ask every week to party is starting to avoid them so obviously direct sales is a scam, and so on and so forth. You can only grin and bear it for so long before you (or I, perhaps?) want to scream!

How on earth do we love the unlovables?

You can ignore them... but they seem to get louder over time. You can pass them on to someone else on your team and hope that she can handle Negative Nancy's personality, but then that consultant may never speak to you again! Shy of pulling out your hair, changing your phone number, and blocking them on social media, what's a girl to do?

You remember when Jesus fed the 5,000 don't you? Do you know what happened after? Jesus and his disciples had gone across the lake to Capernaum. When the crowd he'd fed realized the disciples and Jesus had left, they went searching for them. John 6:25 says,

> "When they found him on the other side
> of the lake, they asked him, 'Rabbi, when
> did you get here?'"

Jesus knew they didn't come to find more about God, or to follow Him as their teacher, and he called them out on it in verse 26.

> "Jesus answered, "Very truly I tell you,
> you are looking for me, not because you
> saw the signs I performed but because
> you ate the loaves and had your fill."

He knew that they just wanted more food! But Jesus told them to stop looking for the food that only filled their bellies, and start looking for the bread of life!

Attitudes and Negative Neds came a'running! They asked him: What sign are you going to give us so we can believe you? What are you going to do for us? Our relatives ate manna! What do you have for us?"

Can you even imagine the audacity? Gimme, gimme, gimme! When Jesus told them that HE was the bread of life–whoa buddy–I can just see the eye-rolling through the pages. The Jews there began to grumble and whisper amongst themselves, saying "Isn't this Joseph's son? Dude, we know your mom and dad! How can you say "I came down from heaven?!"

He told them again in John 6:43-51, "Stop your grumbling! I am the bread of life! This bread of life that you will eat is my flesh, which I will give so that everyone can have life."

Then they argued some more asking, "How can this man give us his flesh to eat?"

Over and over again, he tried to explain to them, and over and over again, they argued and grumbled, and tried to make him look bad, finally saying they just couldn't accept what he'd said. And Jesus said you know what, if you're offended, I'm sorry. I've spoken the truth. The fact that you can't accept it is of your own choosing. His words were full of life, and of the Holy Spirit. Those who didn't believe were CHOOSING not to believe, and the negativity was just an excuse.

John 6:68-69 goes on to tell us that many of Jesus' disciples left him, and no longer followed, and Jesus was okay with that.

> "He asked the twelve "Do you want to leave, too?" and Peter told him "Lord, to whom shall we go? You have the words of eternal life. We have come to believe and to know that you are the Holy One of God."

Even Jesus had people who grumbled about who He was and what He did. They rolled their eyes, said he was a fraud, and they weren't buying what he was sellin'! When Jesus replied to the Negative Neds, he did exactly what he expects US to do: respond in love, speak the truth, hold our temper, and be willing to let them go if the Nancys continue with their bully tactics.

~ Think About It ~

Satan knows how to push your buttons! Like that customer who boldly announces AT your party that she won't buy your handbag because she doesn't buy anything made in China (besides, of course, her cell phone made in China, her Japanese car, and her makeup from London and Canada). Or that downline consultant who just grumbles about why her business isn't working when she spends hours on social media each night. Satan knows their grumbling can make you think less-than-holy thoughts, but don't give in. Who's your Nancy? How do you need to respond to her (or to Negative Ned!) Follow Jesus' example to these Negative Nancys: Speak Truth. In Love. Let Go and focus your efforts on those who DO love your products.

_____

_____

_____

_____

_____

_____

~ Pray About It ~

Dear Lord, You know these Nancys drive me crazy! Remind me when I see Nancy that I need to follow your example in handling the situation. Help me to speak love and truth and not lose my cool. Thank you Lord that for every Negative Nancy, you have provided me with dozens of Positive Pollys that you sent my way to encourage me. Thank you Lord for YOUR belief in my business, and for your belief in ME! ~Amen

More Than Sales

How Would Jesus Lead?

Day 23
Temptation To Do
The Wrong Thing

"But I did obey the Lord," Saul said. "I went on the mission the Lord assigned me. I completely destroyed the Amalekites and brought back Agag their king" (1 Samuel 15:20, NIV).

Every day, we can be tempted to do the wrong thing in our business. Satan can tempt us to take someone else's customers and clients as our own, charge full price when selling product to another consultant in need, even if we've already made commission on it, or cheat a customer out of a few cents on her order. Most of the time, we walk away from these temptations. But what about when the temptation isn't to do something wrong, but rather to not follow God's direction completely?

Israel had just come out of Egypt when they were attacked by the Amalekites. Saul, who was king of Israel at the time, heard this word from the Lord: "Now go, attack the Amalekites and totally destroy everything that belongs to them. Do not spare them;

put to death men and women, children and infants, cattle and sheep, camels and donkeys." So Saul set out to destroy the Amalekites... but instead of killing everything as he was instructed, he spared Agag, the Amalekite king, as well as the best of the sheep, cattle, calves, and lambs. God saw what Saul did, and he said "I am grieved that I have made Saul king, because he has turned from me and has not carried out my instruction."

Meanwhile, Saul was quite proud of himself! He patted himself on the back, and even set to creating a monument in his own honor! When Samuel met up with Saul, Saul said "Hey! What's up? Bless you brother, I did what God asked me to!" But the truth was, he hadn't. God had told him to destroy Amalek, and he not only kept the king alive, he and his army kept the choice cattle and animals for themselves.

Samuel called him out on it, and you know what Saul said? He wasn't sorry. In fact, he never even recognized that he had done wrong in God's eyes. He said "The soldiers did it! It was their idea! Don't worry, they saved the best to give sacrifice to *your* (speaking to Samuel) God, but it's okay, we destroyed the rest." They took the best of the best, and of that, planned to send up a burnt offering to God. And did you notice that Saul called God "*your God*"? His behavior proved that he'd only been giving lip-service to God; our God wasn't *Saul's* God to obey.

More Than Sales

But Samuel knew that only following God a little bit was the same as not following Him at all!

> "What is more pleasing to the Lord: your burnt offerings and sacrifices or your obedience to his voice? Listen! Obedience is better than sacrifice, and submission is better than offering the fat of rams" (I Samuel 15:22, NLT).

God doesn't want our sacrifices, or our halfhearted attempts at running a business. He gives us direction, leads, customers, and orders, and expects us to follow through with them fully, 100%, completely. When we don't, just as He was with Saul, He can be sorry He ever chose us for a task in the first place! How sobering, that a sacrifice, even if it's HUGE and seems like it *should* be pleasing to the Lord doesn't mean as much as simple obedience to the tasks He gives us!

We can pretend to do business all day long, but all God wanted from Saul, and all He wants from us, is a heart of obedience; more than our tithes and more than our after-the-fact sacrifices. When we do obey God with the tasks He's given us, we please Him so much more and enter into that sweet connection we have with Him as our shepherd, leader, friend, savior and business partner.

~ Think About It ~

What instructions has God given me that I've not fully obeyed Him in? Have I grieved Him in anything? Is there somewhere in my–our–business where God is sorry He accepted becoming my business partner? Is there something specific that God asked me to do that I only did halfheartedly?

_____

_____

_____

_____

_____

_____

Those are hard questions to ask; no one wants to think we would make God sorry, but if it can happen to Saul, it can happen to us! Can you trust God enough to ask Him, or would you be afraid of the answer, which may prevent you from asking at all?

~ Pray About It ~

Dear Lord, please show me where I've not followed Your instructions, or give me confirmation that I truly have! Help me understand the true path you have for me, and help me know without a shadow of a doubt that the road I'm taking is directed by you, and not for selfish gain, selfish reasons, or mistaken pride in my own ability to lead myself. Thank you, Lord, that I have you to guide me and bring me so much more success with your path than I could ever have on my own! Amen

Day 24
The Accidental Leader: Leading When You Don't Feel Qualified

"So they inquired further of the Lord, "Has the man come here yet?" And the Lord said, "Yes, he has hidden himself among the supplies" (1 Samuel 10:22, NIV).

I have a girl on my downline whom I'll call "Annie." Annie is fun and very sweet. She works two jobs, and found direct sales by accident. It came naturally to her, and next thing you know, she had recruited someone, and then someone else. Soon, she had a team of 7 ladies and had made one promotion, with a second not far behind.

Annie told me one day that she didn't feel qualified as a leader and was going to quit the business so she wouldn't have to take on the responsibility of helping someone else be successful. She didn't have the time to take on everything she thought she had to do to be a leader. She thought leadership meant you had to have experience first, and be REALLY great at full-time direct sales before you could lead others to be successful. I had told her that wasn't the case, but Annie's fear of leading these women was bigger than her desire to meet her own goals, and she went from leader to hobbyist in one simple month. Annie never did come back to leadership, although I pray she does discover the unlimited potential I think she possesses as a leader.

You know, Saul was the same way. Saul was cute! And tall! A head taller than all the other guys in Jerusalem. Saul was just out in the countryside one day, looking for his father's lost donkeys with his servant. After they'd gone through multiple areas looking for them by foot, his servant suggested they go ask the local man of God which way they should go next. So they did!

Unbeknownst to them, the prophet Samuel knew they were coming! God had told him the night before that at this same time, a man would come from Israel, and that he was God's chosen leader. Samuel was to anoint him as king while he was there. Samuel informed them that the donkeys had been found. He said in I Samuel 9:20,

> "Why are you troubling yourself with these donkeys, when all that is desirable in all of Israel will belong to you and your family?"

Saul was confused. He came from the smallest family in the tribe of Benjamin! Surely this talk was crazy talk! Samuel invited Saul to dinner, and to rest for the night. The next morning, Samuel sent Saul's servant home, then anointed Saul with oil, and told him God had appointed him as leader of the people, and revealed all God had told him, and sent him back home.

Samuel called an assembly of the entire Israeli nation. Samuel knew God had chosen Saul as a leader, and that God would mold him into the leader He wanted Saul to be. Here are all of the tribes of Judah, standing before Samuel, and Samuel announces that Saul, from the tribe of Benjamin, and family of Matri had been chosen as king.

Then, Saul stood tall and proud and said, "Yes! I will gladly be a fair and just king for the people."

JUST KIDDING.

Saul was hiding! You think you're not ready to lead your group of two women, or four women, or eight women? Saul went out looking for donkeys a few days ago, and came back as king over hundreds of thousands of people! When Samuel was ready to introduce him, this man that towered over everyone else by an entire head was hiding in the luggage! Talk about being an accidental leader!

But not everybody believed. 1 Samuel 10:27 says some people scoffed at him and disrespected him.

"How can this man save us?" they said. They despised him and wouldn't bring him presents, but he didn't say anything."

Maybe they didn't believe he could be a good leader. But that doesn't matter! You know who did believe? God believed. And Samuel believed. Just because Saul wasn't aware that God chose him for something greater as a leader doesn't make it not so! And the same is with you.

Not everyone starts as a leader, but with even your first recruit, SOMEBODY said "I want to partner with you." *YOU EXHIBIT* that special something that made her choose you as her business partner over any other person. Don't think she chose you just because you were the one who did her party. You're her leader because God arranged a chance meeting, and GOD believed in your leadership abilities when He placed her on your team.

~ Think About It ~

Do you think of yourself as a leader? Or are you "hiding among the luggage" when GOD assigns someone to your team that He needs to grow and develop, and can only learn those qualities from you? Do you think Satan is well served when God calls you to be a leader and you shrink back into the limelight, doubting your own abilities as well as God's sanity in choosing you? Can you accept that maybe God *did* choose you as a leader, and you are worthy of partnering with your downline to bring out something hidden in them that God wants to shine?

_____

_____

_____

_____

_____

_____

~ Pray About It ~

Dear Jesus, it's hard to think I am the one you want to be in charge of these women. I don't know what I'm doing. I'm scared, and I don't think I have what it takes. I'm not even sure of what I'm doing myself, or if I even want to stay in this business; how can I lead these other women? But I'm trusting you that you have partnered with ME in MY business, and that these are the women you've chosen for me. Help me believe that you have a greater plan that I may not even see, and help me develop myself, and them, to be the businesswomen you want us to be. In Your precious, holy name, Amen.

Day 25
Leading When You Don't Feel Like It

"At once Jesus realized that power had gone out from him. He turned around in the crowd and asked, "Who touched my clothes?" (Mark 5:30, NIV).

I met with a consultant at a local regional team meeting one night. She'd been with our direct sales company for the exact same amount of time that I had, and considered herself a "hobbyist." At first, she told me she didn't really have any goals and didn't want to ever recruit anybody. She didn't have time to be a leader and this was just a part-time gig.

The more we talked, the more I heard her heart. She *wanted* to be "more" but was afraid. Afraid she'd missed the boat, afraid she'd lost her chance, afraid to step out. She was even afraid of me, because my own level in the business reminded her of where she wasn't, since we'd joined at almost the same time. It was easier for her to stay in her comfort zone and tell herself she was happy than it was for her to take a chance, but miss the mark.

As a leader, this stranger broke my heart. Where was her upline? Hadn't they asked her these questions? Didn't they know that deep within she longed to be more? And then I caught the faint whisper of the Holy Spirit. *This girl is someone on YOUR team. Think about them. Who on your team longs for more if YOU would encourage them the way I've planned for you to? Who have you not asked these very same questions to?*

Don't you just hate it when God reaches down, grabs your face in his hands and gets you nose-to-nose like a 2-yr old to get your attention? He's right, you know. I know there are girls on my team who have this very same need that signed as hobbyists, and I have assumed would always stay hobbyists. Our "why" changes daily, why wouldn't we—I—expect theirs to?

There was a man in the Bible named Jairus, whose daughter had been ill and was just about dead. Jesus had been performing miracles, and Jairus came to ask Jesus to come to his house and heal her. As they were walking through the crowds, Jesus felt someone touch the hem of his clothing. It was a woman who had an issue of blood. Today, this woman would be someone who might have fibroid tumors or a heavy menstrual cycle, but at the time, a woman on her cycle was unclean for 7 days. If a person's issue lasted more than seven days, they were thought unclean, period. Here was this woman who had an issue of blood for twelve straight YEARS. Can you even imagine?

She would not have been allowed to go to the temple at that time, and likely lived alone, because she could not be around a man. Everything she touched, sat on, or came in contact with, had to be washed, including people! Any contact at all with her husband (not just sexual) was also unclean during that time and had to be washed. No hugging, no kissing, not even a soft shoulder to cry on. The doctors and medicines of the time could not heal her. Yet she believed Jesus could. She longed to be changed, longed for something more, longed for healing and a fresh start, and she believed HE could give it to her. No one else had been able to fix this, in fact, Mark 5:26 says,

> "She had suffered a great deal under the care of many doctors and had spent all she had, yet instead of getting better she grew worse."

Yet she had come out in *public* because Jesus was here. And as He walked by, she reached out in faith that He could heal her. Mark 5:25-34 continues with this,

> "When she heard about Jesus, she came up behind him in the crowd and touched his cloak because she thought, "If I just touch his clothes, I will be healed."

Immediately her bleeding stopped and she felt in her body that she was freed from her suffering. At once Jesus realized that power had gone out from him.

He turned around in the crowd and asked, "Who touched my clothes?"

"You see the people crowding against you," his disciples answered, "and yet you can ask, 'Who touched me?'"

But Jesus kept looking around to see who had done it. Then the woman, knowing what had happened to her, came and fell at his feet and, trembling with fear, told him the whole truth. He said to her, "Daughter, your faith has healed you. Go in peace and be freed from your suffering."

The minute she did it, he felt power leave his body, and he asked "Who touched me?" Jesus was in a crowd–jostling back and forth–perhaps hundreds had touched him. But her touch was different. It was in faith, reaching out, her only hope. Where everyone else was just a Jesus groupie, her touch was a faith so bold it zapped the power straight from Him into her very being!

Her story was so important that three of the four gospels included her. She was a life who had gone a very long time in the same situation until she reached out to something–someone–that could help her move beyond the place she was. Her story isn't one of why we need to be a leader, but rather, the difference we can make in the life of one woman, when we recognize who is reaching out to us. It is then we align our why with God's heart for our business – to reach other women and give them the opportunity to be all they can be.

~ Think About It ~

Maybe you don't feel like being a leader today. Maybe you don't have time to talk to recruits and team members about their dreams and goals. It could be because you're still under the assumption that it's YOU building the business, not God. He has placed every single person in your path for a reason. He has sent them to *you* to touch the "hem of your garment"– not because you can heal them, but because through you and through your business, they see HIM. If you close your eyes and ask God to bring to mind the one person you need to reach out to, who wants to be more, but is just waiting for the outstretched hand from you, He will. Who is it? When was the last time you reached out to her? Can you reach out to her now?

_____

_____

_____

_____

_____

_____

~ Pray About It ~

Thank you God for showing me who on OUR team needs this business. Forgive me for acting as if I am the one in control of the who, what, when, and why. Give me courage to approach them, and the words to say that will tell them what YOU think of them so they can become all YOU have intended for them to be, not all that I assumed they'd be. Thank you. Lord. for this bouquet of women that you have hand-picked for me, and help me to love and appreciate each flower in my bouquet for the beauty they possess, and the treasures they are. In Your precious, holy name. Amen

Day 26
Left Behind

> "Are not two sparrows sold for a penny? Yet not one of them will fall to the ground outside your Father's care" (Matthew 10:29, NIV).

As I write this—even think on the topic—I could toss my cookies. My head starts pounding, and I find myself catching my breath. I'm going to digress from sales just for a minute and talk about writing. I love it; not a day goes by where I'm not writing something for kids, something for women, for my travel business, for my direct sales team. Every single day.

I have friends who blog. A friend who's written a book—actually, several friends who have written books. Friends who go to writers' conferences. And every time I hear their stories of successes they've had, and places they've gone, I feel like they're leaving me further and further behind. Like they're in a league I'll never reach. It's a desperation deep in my soul; I want so badly to go where they're going! But sometimes I feel the train is leaving without me, and by the time I catch up, they'll be so far ahead, I won't even be on the same track.

I shake that devil off, but then my thoughts drift to my team. We all have women on our team who are rockstars. We all have women who are top sellers, who are number one every single month. If we're lucky, that group of rockstars is 20%. What do YOU think about the remaining 80%? Your upline will tell you–the business will tell you–that you should spend the most time on the ones who make you money. Your effort should match their effort.

What if God invested in US that way? What if He only answered 20% of our prayers? Or listened to only the 20% of Christians that routinely brought new people to Christ? What if He only responded to a certain percentage of Jesus Freaks? The principle is the same; His love is enough to cover EVERYONE on our team. Likewise, running our business with Him as our CEO means that we love everyone too– not just the high sellers. Not just the top in sales.

Chances are, those 80% are thinking every time you recognize the successes of the 20%, the 80 feel further and further behind. When we recognize ONLY the top tier, the remainder feel like it's an impossible feat. Without even knowing it, you've left most of your team behind simply by accident, as the rest of your team train motors on without them.

Your team brings so much to the table; they were brought by God and *placed* on your team to be more than a dollar sign for you! Matthew 10:29-31 says:

More Than Sales

"Are not two sparrows sold for a penny? Yet not one of them will fall to the ground outside your Father's care. And even the very hairs of your head are all numbered. So don't be afraid; you are worth more than many sparrows."

Even the tiny sparrows are loved and *treasured* by our loving father. There is none too small for His concern. That's the way He feels about our entire team. There is none too small for His concern. No minimum sales. No PV requirements. Just a genuine love for us, no matter where we are in our business.

The 80%—the way we keep them from feeling left behind is by making sure they *do* feel included in the journey! Recognizing them for little successes as well as big lets them know that YOU, just like Jesus, care about even the littlest sparrows on your team. Finding a way to recognize even the sparrows will help make sure your entire team soars like eagles!

If that person feeling left out is you, I'll tell you what helps me: Knowing that the plan God has for me has already been identified! It wouldn't matter how many successes my friends rack up, God has plans for me that guarantee I'll never be left behind from the greatest plan of all! The one that's meant for me!

~ Think About It ~

When we focus only on the top sellers and rockstars of our team, we can miss out on connecting with the entire team as a whole. Granted, not everyone will accept your invitation for a group hug 'round the bonfire singing Kumbayah. But those who have felt left out will realize that you truly do care about them, and feel that they bring something to your team that no one else can. Each woman matters to God, and each woman matters to your team. Who on your team needs to hear that today?

~ Pray About It ~

Lord, with so many women on my team, it's hard to recognize every single woman. Thank you Lord that you don't feel that way when you look at me—that you recognize me by sight, even with the millions of other women on the planet! Help me see the women on my team the way YOU see them. Help me develop a system where I can reach out to them the way you want me to. Thank you Lord that you love the sparrows the same way you love the eagles, and help me to love them both the same way too! ~ Amen

When Bad Things Happen

Day 27
Taking The High Road

"Then Peter said, "Ananias, how is it that Satan has so filled your heart that you have lied to the Holy Spirit and have kept for yourself some of the money you received for the land?" (Acts 5:3, NIV).

Every single day, a new consultant is "born" by joining your Direct Sales company. Sometimes she's on your team, and sometimes she's not. Sometimes she's in your town, and sometimes she's across the country. You may never meet this consultant in person, and wouldn't know her if she walked past you in public, but you see her social media posts, you see her obvious disregard for policies and procedures, and you mutter unspeakable things about her under your breath.

That's not the way you want to be, but it's so hard to be the one taking the high road and doing the right thing when these women are advancing their business by sacrificing integrity! The competition is fierce, and every new day there's a potential for someone to steal your clients away to a newer, shinier consultant, who promises big things if they come see her instead.

What's an honest woman to do?

The plain and simple answer is: no matter what, take the high road!

In the days after Jesus' death, all the believers and disciples were "of one heart and mind"; their beliefs were the same, their ideals were the same. They shared everything they had and lived together. No one was needy. In fact, those who had more would share with those who had none, and those who owned homes or land would sell them to provide for the group. Barnabas was one of these men. He sold a field that he owned and laid the profit at the apostles' feet for them to distribute to the entire group.

That was a wonderful thing–an honorable thing–the money was received with joy!

Nearby, a woman names Sapphira and her husband Ananias saw what happened, and how Barnabas was favored after his deed. The two of them plotted to sell a piece of property, and bring part of the money, while keeping a portion secretly hidden for themselves. They brought the money that they'd agreed to give to the apostles' and laid it at their feet.

> "Then Peter said, "Ananias, how is it that Satan has so filled your heart that you have lied to the Holy Spirit and have kept for yourself some of the money you received for the land? Didn't it belong to

More Than Sales

you before it was sold? And after it was sold, wasn't the money at your disposal? What made you think of doing such a thing? You have not lied just to human beings but to God" " (Acts 5:3-4).

They'd been outed! You see, they had done this thing not out of love for the Lord and His people the way Barnabas had; they did it out of envy. Greed. A sheer goal of being recognized, praised, and applauded. Meanwhile, they'd kept a cut for themselves, so that they could live higher than everyone else in the group. God's punishment for them? Death.

> "When Ananias heard this, he fell down and died. And great fear seized all who heard what had happened. About three hours later his wife came in, not knowing what had happened. Peter asked her, "Tell me, is this the price you and Ananias got for the land?"

> "Yes," she said, "that is the price." Peter said to her, "How could you conspire to test the Spirit of the Lord? Listen! The feet of the men who buried your husband are at the door, and they will carry you out also." At that moment she fell down at his feet and died" (Acts 5:5-10).

I'm definitely NOT saying that consultants who are unscrupulous deserve death. I am simply telling you that Barnabas followed the group policies and was rewarded by the apostles' and by God. Ananias and Sapphira took a shady alternative and covered it up with a lie. Their reward was death.

It can be so tempting to call out another consultant for their underhanded ways. But vengeance belongs to God! His desire for us is that we live clean lives, and run honest businesses. He sees every dishonest act, and He alone will be the one to discipline the offenders.

~ Think About It ~

No matter what you see another consultant doing, your responsibility to take the high road is to God and the business you own with Him. Does that mean removing yourself from a group that doesn't always take the high road? Does that mean "breaking up" with another consultant who has been your friend for awhile, but doesn't share your desire to take the high road? It means keeping your eyes on your own business and running it the way God desires, knowing that He'll handle those who aren't running their businesses honestly.

_____

_____

_____

_____

~ Pray About It ~

Lord, it is SO HARD to keep my eyes on my own business when Suzie Seller is doing so well by cheating the rules. Help me see that taking the high road is the only road I need. Remind me to be like Barnabas and to serve you in this business with joy instead of Sapphira, who just longed for spotlight. Thank you, Lord, for the knowledge that YOU and only You are what grows my business. ~ Amen

Day 28
Desperation & Demotions

"These things I remember as I pour out my soul: how I used to go with the multitude, leading the procession to the house of God, with shouts of joy and thanksgiving among the festive throng" (Psalm 42:4, NIV).

AND

"Then I said to them, 'You see the trouble we are in, how Jerusalem lies in ruins with its gates burnt. Come, let us rebuild the wall of Jerusalem, so that we may no longer suffer disgrace'" (Nehemiah 2:17, NIV).

Maybe it hasn't happened to you, but chances are it will happen to someone in your downline. You've watched your team for three months barely squeak by, barely meeting the minimums to keep you active. You are up chewing on your fingernails until 11:59 pm, watching the numbers add up. Then one month, you don't make it. A second month rolled by without making it. And now you're three weeks into your demotion month. It's make it or break it time, and your entire team has 1/10th of the sales they normally have.

Finally, the last day of the month rolls by and it's official; you've demoted.

It's devastating. You think *How can I face my teammates and sisters? Sure, I can recruit 4 more, get them qualified, regain my title, regain my team, but do I even want to?* And you talk yourself out of ever seeking leadership again. You tell yourself it was never meant to be. Slowly, the pain sets in as you look up the team leader Facebook page and see that you've been removed. This is worse than the worst threat of third-grade-cooties. Once you drop down, you might as well drop off the face of the earth, as your upline will never see you as a serious leader worth her time again, right? It's okay, I've heard Satan whisper the lie that there's no reason to get back up again. And David has too.

You see, the psalmist was in a spiritual funk. He longed for the comfort that only God could provide–a place and time that was no more. Psalm 42 tells us,

> "As the deer pants for streams of water, so my soul pants for you, O God. My soul thirsts for God, for the living God. When can I go and meet with God? My tears have been my food day and night, while men say to me all day long, "Where is your God?" These things I remember

as I pour out my soul: how I used to go with the multitude, leading the procession to the house of God, with shouts of joy and thanksgiving among the festive throng."

David knew loss. Where there used to be festive dancing and plenty, there is now *want*. Not only that, people are telling him "Hey, if you really had a god, he would have helped you out of this mess to begin with!"

But David knows better. He doesn't just have *a* god, he has THE God! His reminder to himself is not to be downtrodden, but to praise God in all circumstances, both the highs and the lows, because nothing has happened to him that wasn't overseen by The Lord!

"Why are you downcast, O my soul? Why so disturbed within me? Put your hope in God, for I will yet praise him, my Savior and my God."

He tells us that by day, God shows His love to us, but by night, He gives us a song! Psalm 42:8 goes on to say:

"By day the LORD directs his love, at night his song is with me-- a prayer to the God of my life."

More Than Sales

You see, even as his friends make fun of him, he still gives praise to God. And that's the perfect example for us. Anyone can have a song in the day. Having a song at night; when it's dark, scary, lonely, and gloomy; when you've lost your title, your friends, and your business; maintaining your song in the darkness is what will keep your courage and hope up, and help you fix your eyes on Jesus! His reminder in verse 11 shows us that even though we do have hard times–and we WILL–our God will never leave us. He's in the very business of meeting you exactly where you are, not waiting for you to get to a certain place before He reaches out to you! We can place our hope and trust in Him, the one who will never leave us or forsake us!

Okay. So you fell down. What're you gonna do? Stay there? Or dust yourself off and get up? It's really comfortable down in the heap pile, isn't it? But nothing good happens in the heap pile, and you'll always wonder what might have been.

I hear you. "Karen, why would I even bother rebuilding? If I fell, it happened for a reason."

Yep, sure did. Maybe it was so YOU can empathize when your team mate does the same thing. Maybe it's so you can have an amazing testimony like Nehemiah did.

Nehemiah 1 tells us of the cupbearer for King Artaxerxes I, Nehemiah,

"Hanani, one of my brothers, came from Judah with some other men... they said to me, "Those who survived the exile and are back in the province are in great trouble and disgrace. The wall of Jerusalem is broken down, and its gates have been burned with fire." When I heard these things, I sat down and wept. For some days I mourned and fasted and prayed before the God of heaven" (Neh. 1:2-4).

Jerusalem was the home of Nehemiah's forefathers and hearing of its desolation broke his heart. When it was time for him to serve the King, Artaxerxes noticed Nehemiah's heavy heart. Nehemiah had prayed to the Lord that he would have favor in the king's eyes, as he told Artaxerxes about his thought to rebuild the wall of the city. He wanted nothing from the people of the kingdom, no favors, other than a letter asking for safe keeping as Nehemiah traveled, which was granted. There were enemies that heard of Nehemiah's plan; in fact, they plotted to overthrow the effort!

"And our enemies said, 'They will not know or see anything before we come upon them and kill them and stop the work.' When the Jews who lived near them came, they said to us ten times,

'From all the places where they live they will come up against us' " (Neh 4:11-12).

But our God's support can make ANYTHING happen! With the help of the people, Nehemiah was a true leader to the people; he directed their efforts, and organized the people so they could rebuild the wall and protect the city. Half of the workers were building the wall, while the other half were on patrol to guard the city from those plotting to destroy it. In fact, at one point, the workers even carried their loads so that one hand did the word, and the other hand carried a weapon!

Their hearts, their minds, their ambitions; they were one solid unit, with one solid purpose–rebuilding that which was lost; that which was broken, burned, and destroyed.

Fifty-two days was all it took them to rebuild the entire wall around the city, with the help of a mighty God. An entire city wall built in 52 days, without the machinery we have today, simply because *God Helped*. That same God is ready and waiting to help YOU rebuild that which is destroyed, burnt, and lying in ruins.

~ Think About It ~

Demotions and disappointments are nothing that our God can't help us overcome. Dealing with loss in your business is hard. You've poured your very soul into your customers and clients, your downline and your teammates. Losing all or even part of that can leave a huge emotional void. I know it's heartbreaking, but it's not the end of the world, unless you let it be!

There is healing in knowing that *God still values you*, even if you did get removed from a certain group, or didn't meet an incentive. There is hope in realizing that the same God who helped you build this business from the get-go is there to help you RE-build it, IF you'll let Him. There is POWER in knowing that God is NOT done with you yet–not in your business, and not in your walk with Him! Where can you start fresh with God today, empowered to build something mighty, something God-filled, something AMAZING?

_____
_____
_____
_____
_____
_____

~ Pray About It ~

Lord, I have felt so defeated. Ready to throw in the towel. Make me like Nehemiah; full of faith that your ability to help me rebuild is greater than any fear I have of my own inabilities to pick up a single brick. I need your help. I am ready to rebuild and my hope is reborn in you! Help me build something AMAZING for your glory! ~ Amen

Day 29

Just When You Think You've Got It All Together

"Be alert and of sober mind. Your enemy the devil prowls around like a roaring lion looking for someone to devour" (1 Peter 5:8, NIV).

Just as soon as you make God your business partner, guess what you do at the same time? You put a target on your back for Satan to trip you up! You see, entering into a new partnership with God makes God so happy! At the same time, it makes Satan jealous. He's already upset that you're a child of God and he can't steal your salvation away. Now you're business partners with God? Oh no, that'll never do! So guess what's now on Satan's list-of-things-to-do?

Drive. You. CRAZY!

He'll make you doubt your purpose, and your effectiveness in leading others to Jesus... whisper your weaknesses into your ear, and stir up drama within your team. He'll tempt you to conduct shady business practices, or work in other areas of your life that cause you to take your focus off your business. He can also cause you to put other priorities in the wrong order so that your focus is ONLY on your business, allowing your family and other relationships to suffer.

What's a girl to do?

First, remember the order in which we were created way back in Adam and Eve days. First up was a relationship with God, then came family, then work. God's heart and plan for your business will never be to put it first, above Him. But the temptation to put business first is still there because we see the end result of our lives as a successful leader, as something God would want for us.

Let me explain. Maybe your end goal is to be a stay-at-home mom and quit your corporate job. Maybe it's to build an orphanage in Uganda. Maybe it's just to be able to afford to tithe for the first time, or pay for private school for your son. Surely, God wants these things too, right?

One would think so. But the things God wants MOST for you are those priorities that God already laid out in the perfect order... a relationship with him, a relationship with your family, then work. Don't forget that, because when Satan comes a'knocking— and he will—who you are in Christ, and your family members will be what will lift you lift you back up.

Take Job, for instance. When Job was being tempted, he had EVERYTHING. He was very wealthy, had a wonderful family, and was a successful businessman. Satan was already looking for someone to destroy, and God knew Job's heart was so devoted that even the worst brought on from Satan couldn't shake Job's faith. He said in Job 1:

> "The LORD said to Satan, "Where have you come from?"

(Oh come now, you don't think Jesus didn't know where Satan was, do you? Of course He did!)

> "Satan answered the LORD, "From roaming through the earth and going back and forth in it." Then the LORD said to Satan, "Have you considered my servant Job? There is no one on earth like him; he is blameless and upright, a man who fears God and shuns evil" (Job 1:2-3).

You see, Satan roams the entire earth LOOKING for people to destroy. Actively looking. It's not something he reserved for people on the earth thousands of years ago. He does it every day and he enlists his minions in his war as well. We can't be so naive to think that we're exempt from temptation simply because we're Christians. In fact, it's the opposite. Because we *do* love God, Satan is on the prowl for us. Don't let your business be a place open for Satan to wreak havoc.

The great thing is, the One who lives in us has power over Satan. But that's not our doing–it's God's

More Than Sales

doing. When Jesus was teaching on earth, He would send 72 of his disciples ahead of him as they entered the towns to teach. Luke 10:17-20 says:

> "The seventy-two returned with joy and said, "Lord, even the demons submit to us in your name."
> Jesus replied, 'I saw Satan fall like lightning from heaven. I have given you authority to trample on snakes and scorpions and to overcome all the power of the enemy; nothing will harm you. However, do not rejoice that the spirits submit to you, but rejoice that your names are written in heaven.'"

See, we're not to be proud that we hold the power to destroy Satan. According to Jesus, what's even *more* important is our relationship to God–the very one who GIVES us that power! We put that above *everything* else. Our businesses must supplement that relationship... not take the place of it.

As we become more and more successful, it's easier to think that our success is from something we're doing right, or place our position up on a pedestal because "we" earned it. Or even worse, to brush God aside while we work even harder to stay on top. That pride is our *own* abilities is exactly what Satan will use to try and trip us up like he did with Job!

But like Job knew, and like Jesus told the 72, our relationship with God is worth ALL of those "things"!

The closer you get to God, and the closer you get to finding out who you are in Christ, the more aware you have to be of Satan's plans to trip you up! When you think you have it all together, Satan will be waiting. (But guess what, I've read that story, and I know who wins in the end!) Remember who you are in Christ, who lives *inside* of you! Answer that temptation with a confident heart, knowing God's got your back in every circumstance Satan could dream up.

~ Think About It ~

Can you recall a time where Satan tried to tempt you into making a poor choice? Have you felt a heavy weight to make a wrong decision or even (temporarily) put your priorities in the wrong order to get ahead? If not you, is there a direct sales sister or team member who may need to be reminded that Satan's plans to destroy them will never amount to God's plans for their lives?

_____

_____

_____

_____

_____

_____

~ Pray About It ~

Lord, thank you that you are superior to Satan.
Thank you for giving me the power to speak your
name against the powers that work for my demise.
Remind me Lord when I forget, that it is YOU who is
superior to all. I am so humble to think that the one
who is Master of everything could want to reach
down and hold me in YOUR hand, take my hand.
Not just to be my business partner, but to be my
Father, my Savior, and my friend. Thank you, Lord,
for Jesus, who came to earth to write MY name in
your Book of Life. ~ Amen

Beyond Sales

Day 30
Ho Ho Ho... NO!

"As the man went eastward with a measuring line in his hand, he measured off a thousand cubits and then led me through water that was ankle-deep" (Ezekial 47:3, NIV).

I first learned about Jesus when I was 5 and living with my grandmother. She was disabled, so we didn't go to a brick-and-mortar church, but she made sure we watched church on tv every week. The big white board in my mind that contained the idea of who God was to me had started with "Savior"–that's what I knew Him as! Jesus loves the little children–and that meant me–woo hooo!!

The preacher we watched was all about hellfire-and-damnation so as I grew up and started attending an actual church and learning more about the stories in the Bible, I thought of God as a bit of a mafia boss. "Love me or ELSE!" The white board in my mind seemed to have two very different words for God. "Nice Jesus" for kids, and then "mafia boss" once I was a teenager and grown.

Mafia Boss

I admit, I didn't really know *who* God was. The pastor there was wonderful; very soft spoken and an amazing heart for people. But as a teenager seeking a place to fit in, I listened to Satan tell me all the reasons why church wasn't that place—even though I didn't even really know who Satan was either! And then I stopped going altogether.

It wasn't until I was an adult years later that I started to learn truly who God was. It's almost like I stood on the edge of an ocean that entire time, watching the waves roll in, assuming that the depth of the water that touched my feet was how deep the water was as far as I could see. I knew there was something more; something deeper, and something greater about God, and I wanted to go wherever that was!

Fast forward a bit to life in those early adult years—it was pretty awesome. We'd moved to the South to be near my husband's friends and family, and because the housing market was a lot better for a young couple looking for their first home. I'd found a sweet little church that God himself invited me to, via a little gift bag left on my door. That gift bag left on my doorstep had a letter telling me to "come exactly as I was," which was the very weapon that Satan had used to take me out of the church years ago. As a member of this new church, I'd given my life back to God, and vowed to be and do whatever He wanted with my life. It was a beautiful place to be.

Surrounded by Godly women, I started to scratch the surface of who God was. My grandmother had amazing faith; I knew from her to trust Him and believe in Him, but I didn't really know within my soul who *"Him"* was! These women–they knew Him as so much more than I did–and I wanted to be where they were! I'd prayed for simple pleasures, like a house, or a job for my husband, healing from sickness, to ease the load at work, or to make the right decisions for my own career.

The white board in my mind had always held God as one thing until now. "Nice Jesus", aka Savior was erased, and in its place, "Mafia Boss" had been written. Now, I could erase "Mafia Boss" and replace it with Provider.

Provider

Thinking of God as my provider was wonderful! Provider could mean being a food and needs provider, or a provider of comfort and peace.

Provider was the first and ultimate, multifaceted word for me in learning who God was because there were so many ways that could be applied! It didn't mean ONE thing, like Protector, when He protected me in a car accident from harm. It didn't just have one meaning.

Here at this church, I also began to not just take FROM God, but to give back TO Him as well! I served in Sunday School, children's church, choir, and a host of opportunities. Serving God was FUN at my church, and it never felt like an obligation. All the while I'd continue to seek God for His will for my life. Sometimes, I really was seeking His will. Other times I *thought* I was seeking His will, but what I was really doing was seeking His approval for *my* will for my life.

And there's a big difference. You see, when we think of God as our provider, sometimes He becomes:

Cosmic Santa

My prayers, and even my service, were for me or for those in my immediate circle and friends at church, but they didn't reach far beyond my own desires, contacts, and communities. They were "God, I want...," "God, help me...," and "Lord please..." The

Big Cosmic Santa in the sky loved me and wanted to provide for me, right? Wrong.

Here's the thing. He does love us and wants to provide for us. But He is NOT a Cosmic Santa. God is so much more than we can even imagine. In fact, that big white board that used to be capable of having just one word on it at a time describing who God was for me? As I grew to know him over the years I've never erased a word. I just keep adding.

When God became more to me than just one thing, my desire to know Him even more–to go deeper–grew too. My prayers would reach beyond my immediate circle to people I didn't even know but wanted to help. When I started in direct sales, it grew again. From prayers for women several layers deep on my team, to sending a dollar to a woman I'd never met and never WOULD meet. My desire to serve God went from helping in my church to praying for and helping women not just on my team, but across continents.

In Ezekial 47, Ezekial was given a vision where he was shown a beautiful temple. He was walking with God and being led to a river that surrounded the temple. Everything the river touched was given life.

> "As the man went eastward with a measuring line in his hand, he measured off a thousand cubits and then led me through water that was ankle-deep. He measured off another thousand cubits and led me through water that was knee-deep. He measured off another thousand and led me through water that was up to the waist. He measured off another thousand, but now it was a river that I could not cross, because the water had risen and was deep enough to swim in — a river that no one could cross."

Ezekial could have stayed at the edge of the water, but God was with him and led him in to touch the water, then go deeper, then deeper still. When I first knew *of* God, I barely had touched the water. But I have gone from the edge of the water into the ocean, and this is what I hear.

"Go Deeper."

In this book, we are asking God to be our business partner. But if the white board in *your* mind has only one word for God on it, that might seem impossible. Direct sales is a huge leap of faith–I can go weeks knowing I am right where I need to be, then transition to asking God for the 50th time that same day "But are you *sure?*" You see, each time I ask God to walk with me, *I have to walk, too.* He can't walk alone. When I trust in Him and take His hand, I have to move as well.

These 30 days you've walked with God... are you in deep? Or is God out in the ocean waiting for you while you're still wading in the ankle-deep water? Do you believe that God can be all He is and all He has done, not just for the people in this devotional book, not just for your business, but for *YOUR LIFE?*

~ Think About It ~

He is not a Cosmic Santa; Ho, Ho, NO! He is everything on my white board for me, and more. And if you have just one word on your white board for who God is in your life, go deeper with God, and discover who He really is. I challenge you to start here and think of the words that God is to you. Not just the words everyone else says He is. But who He is and has been to YOU. Write them here, but don't let that end with these six lines. Write in the margin. Write in your Bible. Stick sticky notes to your bathroom mirror so you can see them before you leave each day. Keep them as the screen background on your phone. Whatever you need to remind you of not just who God is but how far He wants to take you in this journey with Him.

_____

_____

_____

_____

_____

_____

~ Pray About It ~

Father God, thank you that you cannot be limited by who we think you are. Thank you that while you are Provider and Father, that's not ALL you are. My mind cannot wrap around the fact that while you are being all of these things for me and I have all of these needs from you, your desires for me are just to walk deeper with you. I know that when I do that Lord, every other desire you have for me is revealed. Thank you, Lord, for already being everything I could ever need. ~Amen

More Than Sales

Day 31
A Life Of Captivity

"We demolish arguments and every pretension that sets itself up against the knowledge of God, and we take captive every thought to make it obedient to Christ" (2 Corinthians 10:5, NIV).

We often think of a life of captivity as being a terrible thing. Sometimes it is, like when a missionary is jailed in a foreign country for speaking to others about Christ, or when animal hoarders keep thirty-seven malnourished dogs caged up in a backyard.

Captivity isn't always bad, however. When oil spills occur off the coast of the US, local birds and sea life are taken into captivity so they can be rescued, cleaned, and rehabilitated. A newborn infant on his way home from the hospital is held captive in the security of the five-point safety harness of his car seat. Endangered animals can be taken into captivity to protect the species and prevent their complete extinction. Captivity can be defined in its most simplest form, as being held under control. 2 Corinthians 10:5 says,

"We demolish arguments and every pretension that sets itself up against the knowledge of God, and we take captive every thought to make it obedient to Christ."

To take something into captivity—to overcome something and bring it under your control—means we must be stronger than it is, be unafraid to take charge. This includes our thoughts.

God made us as free-thinking creatures. This is why there are so many different denominations, theologies, and world views–because none of us are clones of God. We're made in His image, but none of us are exactly the same. Our thoughts are a mixture of our personal history, our experiences, and our influences. All of that makes up who we are. God understands that, but He wants our biggest influence to be HIM!

You see, every one of the doubts you've read throughout this book could have been a thought whispered in your *own* ear by Satan. Whether it's "I can't," or "My upline is terrible," or "My team and customers hate me," they're all incorrect because they are the exact opposite of the truths that God whispers in your other ear, and writes on your heart. HE says "You can." HE says "Love them and learn from them anyway." HE says "I hand-picked you for them, don't give up yet." Our thoughts are just like the birds covered in oil from the spill. If we allow Satan's lies, or even our own self-condemnation to cover us, our soul can become damaged. But if we take captive that destroying thought, we hold the power in Christ to become all that He has for us. Reach out and grab those thoughts, YANK them from Satan's grasp, rescue them, and keep them held close, far from the reach of the one determined to destroy us and keep us from our destiny in Christ.

Victorious women of the Bible were victorious when they listened to God, not their own doubts, doubts from their families, or edicts from kings or higher-ups. Rahab, Sarah, Ruth, Esther... these women, and so many others—even women who surround you today—were great because they defied the logic of what *should* have been. They placed their faith in their God, determined to go only where He was, and walked into their destiny. Thoughts they held captive became a life held captive, a life held safe in the palm of the hand who created us all.

~ Think About It ~

Take captive every thought. Do not let small talk convince you of your worth. Do not let small whispers talk you out of becoming the woman God wants you to be. Do not let naysayers talk you out of your destiny in Christ. Take those thoughts captive, and compare them to God's truths for you. God's plan for you. And God's heart for you. You know exactly what thoughts you need to reach out and grab before they even wind their way into your ear. Capture them, turn them over to Christ, and use the true thoughts of God to take this business to the destiny He has for you!

_____

_____

_____

_____

_____

_____

~ Pray About It ~

When I sat down to write this prayer section, I realized I couldn't. I wanted you to slam this book shut, ready to run out in the street in your metal armor, viking hat, and spear, declaring victory in your business. When I tried to write this prayer... I knew it wasn't mine to say or write. It is yours. You see, only YOU AND GOD know what thoughts you need to take captive. So this section is for you and your Savior to get down and dirty, heart-to-heart. Trust me, He knows anyway, but He's waiting on you to tell him! Go ahead and knock on His door. He's been expecting you.

Those First Four Devotions
Mission: Possible

These first four devotions are what set the wheels in motion for *More Than Sales.* The subject was Mission: Possible, and our focus verse was: With God all things are possible.

I stopped to think about all of the background "noise" that makes things impossible in our own eyes and narrowed those down to four things. Fear, doubt, self-confidence, and self were the four enemies that needed to be identified and conquered to turn our mission from impossible to possible! One day is devoted to each topic. May they help you go from the Impossible to the Possible too!

Mission Possible Enemy #1: DOUBT

Learn: Matthew 19:26 – "With God all things are possible."

Your mission, should you choose to accept it Dream Team, is to use the next few days to identify and conquer the things in your life that make success seem imPossible.

Enemy #1: Doubt

> "When the Philistines heard that David had been crowned king of Israel, they tried to capture him; but David was told that they were coming and went into the stronghold. The Philistines arrived and spread out across the valley of Rephaim. Then David asked the Lord, 'Shall I go out and fight against them? Will you defeat them for me?'" (2 Sam 5:17-19).

We all wonder if God will be there in our time of need, just as David did. "Will you defeat them for me?" he asked. David had good reason to doubt God's ability to protect him – he had people after his head!

When you are about to enter your destiny, Satan seems ready and waiting with his schemes to prevent you from fulfilling that destiny. When David was anointed king of Israel, God's destiny for him was revealed for everyone–even Satan. So, of course, Satan's response was to rally the Philistines, not just to try and kill David, but to defeat David's destiny, and end the prophecies of old.

David did two things that we need to notice. First, he retreated to his stronghold. It was a place of protection and a quiet place. For us, this could be a closet, our bedroom, or wherever we go when life overwhelms us. Second, he talked to God, and asked God for a response. Sometimes we remember to offload our problems, but need to be mindful of His response. In David's stronghold, he asked God for the strategy to defeat his enemy. God revealed it to him and he went on to defeat the Philistines. Go figure, David NEVER lost a battle. Why? Because he learned to ask God for the strategy to defeat his enemies. What if we never lost a daily battle because we asked God first how we can defeat the struggle? What is God waiting to conquer for you, if only you'd ask Him to help?

There are times we doubt God's ability to care FOR us, and his ability to care ABOUT us. Sometimes I think God's silence means that He's not listening, and that's my cue to take matters into my own hands. Oh, and then there's the path I choose when I think I've heard an answer from God but it's really just me. We all know what happens to those who take matters into their own hands. They interpret a direction they believe is from God and head down the wrong path entirely. How many decisions that are documented in the Bible were made by people who took matters into their own hands because God didn't give them an immediate answer to His knowledge of their future? Was it Abraham and Hagar (Gen 16)? Or perhaps it was Rebecca and Jacob? Did God have other plans, other means for fulfilling His will for Jacob that did not involve lying and deception? Of course He did.

Sarah and Rebecca both fell victim to the same problem I sometimes encounter. The it-hasn't-happened-yet-so-God-must-have-changed-His-mind syndrome. That combined with the we-can't-trust-our-Lord-to-provide-the-means-to-make-it-happen disease turned out to be a terrible combination for both of them. Sarah and Rebecca both took matters into their own hands because the outcome that God predicted seemed unreachable by their human hands. What obstacles seem unreachable in your life by your own hands?

If you're still not sure what God would have you do, don't be like Sarah, Rebecca, and Jacob. Rather than taking matters into your own hands, just wait. David was hidden in the stronghold, so if he wasn't sure of God's direction, he could have stayed there safely. 2 Peter 3:8 says,

> "With the Lord, a day is like a thousand years, and a thousand years like a day.

More Than Sales

The Lord is not slow in keeping His promise, as some understand slowness."

Be patient, and truly wait on the Lord, because he does care for you, and about you, even to the tiniest detail. Isaiah 40:27-31 says,

> "Why would you ever complain, O Jacob, or, whine, Israel, saying, "God has lost track of me. He doesn't care what happens to me"? [sic] ...Haven't you been listening? God doesn't come and go. God lasts. He's Creator of all you can see or imagine. He doesn't get tired out, doesn't pause to catch his breath. And he knows everything, inside and out. He energizes those who get tired, gives fresh strength to dropouts. For even young people tire and drop out, young folk in their prime stumble and fall. But those who wait upon God get fresh strength. They spread their wings and soar like eagles, They run and don't get tired, they walk and don't lag behind."

Are you involving God in your business? Are you asking Him to show you the strategies for success, or are you simply hoping to get there eventually?

~ Think About It ~

How have you been doubting God's ability to provide for you? What are you afraid to give to him because you think He can't (or won't) handle it? Think about it, and then confess aloud in your quiet time with the Lord what you haven't been able to trust Him with.

Mission Possible Enemy #2: FEAR

Learn: Matthew 19:26 – "With God all things are possible."

Your mission, should you choose to accept it Dream Team, is to use the next few days to identify and conquer the things in your life that make success seem imPossible.

Enemy #1: Fear

Fear can consume us in our lives and our businesses–fear of calling the customer who needs to make a return. Fear of making booking calls. Fear of rejection. Fear of not taking a leadership class because you don't know if you're cut out for it. Fear of failure. Fear of letting yourself down, your family, your upline, or your team. Fear of leaving your kids while you go to parties. Fear of speaking in public, fear of not seeming intelligent, or not knowing all of the answers.

But fear is not godly. Think about your obstacles, and how God expects you to need help from him. If our lives were very easy, would we need God? Sometimes our valleys are allowed just so we can turn to God and ask for His help. Think about Ruth, the Moabitess. After her husband died, she made the choice to return with her mother-in-law, Naomi, to the city of Bethlehem. I know you've heard that story before, and living with your MIL may be insane enough for some! Then you realize that the Moabites (Ruth's people) were hated by the Israelites. Don't you think Ruth feared the possibility of rejection from Naomi's people? Yet what she saw in Naomi, and the God of Naomi was enough to set aside her fear and follow her newfound faith. Because of her obedience, she ended up with the opportunity of a lifetime by marrying a godly man named Boaz, and having a child who became the grand-father of King David! How do you think her life would be different if she let fear consume her?

Throughout time, God has asked people to step out of their comfort zone – and facing your fears is one way of doing that. What impossibility is standing in your way? And what about Peter? When Jesus called Peter out on the water with him, Peter didn't start to fear until he put his focus on himself and his circumstances, rather than the one who was holding his hand. Is fear holding you back? Are you too afraid to step out of the boat? God's word tells us over and over to "fear not". It's pretty direct. Not "it's okay to be scared", but an order to fear NOT. When we step back into the boat because we're afraid, we're missing out on something glorious that God has ahead for us. Isn't that what faith is – trusting your needs, your cares, and your fears to the only one who can help you overcome them?

~ Think About It ~

Where have you been holding back out of fear? Can you confess aloud to God in your quiet time today what that fear is, and ask for His help to overcome it?

NOT GOOD ENOUGH

Learn: Matthew 19:26 – "With God all things are possible."

Your mission, should you choose to accept it Dream Team, is to use the next few days to identify and conquer the things in your life that make success seem imPossible.

Enemy #3: I'm Not Good Enough

It's easy to see the success of other women and compare yourselves to them. Throughout our entire life we are taught to compete. From ballgames and cheer squads in grade schools, to standardized tests, GPAs and even familial comparisons between you, your siblings, or your cousins. So when we look at our business, we see ourselves in a race with another consultant… to a title… to a number on your team… or to a pv level. We all want to hear our name in lights because we "won" whatever is up for grabs that month. And when we lose, it's also easy to kick ourselves and think that not only is it not for me this time, it will never be for me. "That blessing's not for me. That's someone else's blessing. I'll never be good enough for that."

Stop and think… have you asked for these things? In Numbers 26, the Lord told Moses to divvy up land according to the tribes. In that time, the land was inherited by sons. But Zelophehad "had no sons" to inherit his portion. So instead, his daughters boldly came forth and spoke to Moses, Eleazar the priest, the leaders, and all the congregation and said,

> "Our father died in the wilderness... and he had no sons. Why should the name of our father be taken away from his clan because he had no son? Give to us a possession among our father's brothers" (Num 27:3-4, ESV).

The sisters not only questioned Moses, but they also approached to question God!

They knew that without a brother, they wouldn't receive their fair portion. Their father lived a good life, he was not a rebel, and they knew they deserved to question the status quo, and ask for God's favor.

> "The Lord came back to Moses and said "The daughters of Zelophehad are right in what they are saying; you shall indeed let them possess an inheritance among their father's brothers and pass the inheritance of their father on to them. You shall also say to the Israelites, 'If a man dies, and has no sons, then you shall pass his inheritance on to his daughters. If he has no daughters, then you shall give his inheritance to the nearest kinsman of his clan, and he shall possess it. It shall be for the Israelites a statute

and ordinance, as the LORD commanded Moses'" (Num 27, NRSV).

These women not only changed their own fate, but changed the fate of every woman from that point forward. What would their life be like if they had listened to Satan tell them "just forget it and move on. You're not worthy. You'll never be good enough."

I suppose he spoke the same lies to the Samaritan woman at the well. Jesus had stopped and spoken to her, and asked her for a drink. This woman was the worst of society – she had five husbands, AND a current affair going on at the moment. Not to mention Samaritans were not supposed to even be speaking to Jews. She was drawing water at the hottest part of the day – why? Because she knew she would meet fewer people that way, and would avoid the stares, pointing, and gossip from the townsfolk. But Jesus knew she was worthy, no matter how the rest of society made her feel, and she went back to spread the word and make believers. John 4:39-42, (NIV) says,

> "Many of the Samaritans from that town believed in him because of the woman's testimony, "He told me everything I ever did." So when the Samaritans came to him, they urged him to stay with them, and he stayed two days. And because of his words many more became believers.

They said to the woman, 'We no longer believe just because of what you said; now we have heard for ourselves, and we know that this man really is the Savior of the world.'"

All of these women changed not only their own fates, but the lives and fates of others, by simply believing GOD rather than Satan. They did not believe the whispers that Satan told them. Satan uses those same whispers to try to defeat the missions we have today.

~ Think About It ~

Have you ever felt not good enough in comparison to another consultant? What about to another woman? Have you ever felt that you just don't measure up? In your quiet time, take a moment to reflect on how God truly feels about you. You are unique, and not made for comparison to anyone or anything. Psalm 139:13-16 says,

> "For you created my inmost being; you knit me together in my mother's womb."

Realize that YOU can bring God so much joy, not because you deserve it or because you earned it. There are no levels with God, and no comparisons – you are his child, and Zephaniah 3:17 says,

"He will take great delight in you; in his love he will no longer rebuke you, but will rejoice over you with singing."

Reflect on your own path, whether it's been winding or straight, and realize that God had a reason for sending you this way. Realizing that your journey is your own, with no comparisons to anyone else's journey, how can you start today, to realize you hold the Possible in your hand?

My Biggest Obstacle: ME!

Learn: Matthew 19:26 – "With God all things are possible."

Your mission, should you choose to accept it Dream Team, is to use the next few days to identify and conquer the things in your life that make success seem imPossible.

Enemy #4: Me

Let's face it, sometimes we are our own worst enemy. Maybe we don't have concerns with doubts, or fear, or comparing ourselves to others. Sometimes, the difference between imPossible and Possible is us. Our failure to plan, or inconsistency, or the choices we make to put something off until tomorrow can be devastating. I'm not talking about downtime. Every leader should schedule time for herself, and time for her family. I'm talking about what you do when you you're supposed to be doing something.

Let's say from 7-8 pm, you should be making customer calls. Instead, you're zoned out in front of the tv. Or maybe playing an exciting game of Words with Friends. Maybe you're on Facebook. Or maybe you don't really feel like doing those booking calls, or party prep, so you do some actual work on project B, which isn't really due for another couple days. But it's okay, right, because Project B still needs to be done. Right? Or have you just set yourself up for failure by not doing what you should?

We can procrastinate or put off what should be done, or "do the wrong thing" in many ways. Maybe it's in our business. Maybe it's in our fellowship with God. Maybe it's knowing God as our personal savior to begin with. Did you resolve to read through the Bible this year, and stop somewhere around Genesis 5? Maybe it's with our kids – have you ever said "in a minute" and that minute never came? Maybe you promised them "tomorrow?" Did "tomorrow" ever come? Sometimes procrastination stems from laziness. Know that God favors your hard work (Proverbs 12:24; 13:4) and warns against laziness (Proverbs 15:19; 18:9).

Sometimes it comes from having too much on our plate. Whether it's laziness, busyness, or just choosing to do something other than what we should, the problem is us.

Take Mary and Martha for example. Luke 10:38-42 says,

> "Now as they went on their way, Jesus entered a village. And a woman named Martha welcomed him into her house. And she had a sister called Mary, who sat at the Lord's feet and listened to his teaching. But Martha was distracted with much serving. And she went up to him and said, "Lord, do you not care that my sister has left me to serve alone? Tell her then to help me." But the Lord answered

her, "Martha, Martha, you are anxious and troubled about many things, but one thing is necessary. Mary has chosen the good portion, which will not be taken away from her."

Martha had good intentions. People needed to be served, food needed to be dispersed, the cleaning needed to be done. Martha felt like what she needed to do was important. And yes, her job was important too, but complaining didn't solve the problem. Jesus told her in no uncertain terms to do what was important for the moment, to savor life, and not just do the busywork.

There are women out there whose lives need a change. Maybe it's through income, through the friendships they will make, through the new strongholds in their life, through the prayer warriors interwoven throughout your company, or maybe even to catch a glimpse of a God they may never have heard about through our home-grown faith-based company. Maybe we are the key to that change, and holding off on doing our own work may affect theirs as well. Our job today is simply to persevere, to press on (Philippians 3:13-14), to share our business with them, as well as our faith. Our job is, in fact, to run the race completely. To give our very best, and to not give up today, fearless for tomorrow, knowing that God can handle every problem we have. Matthew 6:34 tells us

"Therefore do not worry about tomorrow, for tomorrow will worry about itself. Each day has enough trouble of its own."

For ourselves, for our families, and for our teams, we must work hard and press on about the tasks we have been given.

~ Think About It ~

What is that one thing in your life that you put off doing? If you could ask your husband and children the same question about you, what would they say? And lastly, if you could ask God that same question about you, what would He say? Look with fresh eyes to see how God can give you the strength to conquer it, and how God can help you make better use of your life to make the impossible POSSIBLE!

The Outsiders

The Outsiders

Do you ever notice people looking at you when your Direct Sales friends get together? Especially when there's lots of laughter and fun? You feel outsiders looking at you... wanting in, but not knowing how to get there? You may not even realize they're there watching you, longing for what you have.

Sometimes Christianity is that way. Women of faith can be *many different* religions. Catholic, Jewish, Baptist. God doesn't have a checklist to ask you what your religion is before you can have a relationship with Him. Like Rahab, Noah, Joseph, David, and Mary Magdalene, God chooses ordinary people to do the most miraculous things – sometimes even people who AREN'T mainstream Christianity.

So what about the direct sales professional who says "But Karen, I can't give this business over to Him, because I don't KNOW Him." And I get it. I hear YOU. My heart is for YOU, the one who doesn't know how to talk to God, or who doesn't think that miracle-sized faith still happens today... for the direct sales consultant in a faith-based company who isn't even sure of her own faith, she just likes the products. She may be just like the outsider, watching a group of direct sales ladies having a blast, and not really sure how to get from where she is to where they are. She may be a Christian, a Muslim, a Hindu, or just might be the person in a faith-based company who believes in God, but has never talked to him, and reading this book was so very hard for her.

She may be you.

Take heart. God wants everyone to know him —even her, and yes, even you. If you are that person who has never spoken to God, who skimmed over the prayer section of each devotional day because that's just not "you," but you are left with more questions now than you ever had… turn to God. He doesn't just want to be the CEO and owner of your business, he wants to be the owner of your heart! He wants you to be his Princess, the daughter of the King. That longing and questioning you feel may just be that He is knocking at the door of your heart, asking if you have room for him there.

You see, no one is getting into heaven without realizing and admitting we are imperfect sinners who are not worthy of going to heaven when we die without Him. God sent his son to earth from heaven to die for us, as an exchange. Because he died, if we accept that exchange and that sacrifice, we have the gift of never dying spiritually and living forever in heaven. But if we don't accept that gift of God saving us through his son Jesus' death, then we'll forever be in hell, a terrible, horrible place, chased and tormented by Satan. For some it's an easy choice, for others it takes an entire lifetime.

God doesn't have different levels of relationships that he wants with us – he longs for ALL

More Than Sales

of us to be close to him. But here's how it starts. Admit we are sinners. Believe that God has an exchange for you, in the form of his son Jesus who died on a cross for our sins. Ask for that forgiveness and for him to be your savior. Believe that you have it! Walk away changed, FOREVER written in the Lamb's (Jesus) Book of Life and be ready to tell someone!

If you've already asked Jesus to be your savior, that's awesome! Did you know that when you're saved—not sprinkled, baptized, or even dedicated—when YOU ask God to come into your heart to save you from eternal death, he literally does! He sends a piece of himself, called the Holy Spirit, to live in us, guide us, and comfort us. He lives in you FOREVER, no matter what Satan will try to tell you!

But even better, because the Holy Spirit is PART of God, you can always have the ability to hear, talk to, and understand God—because that part of Him inside of you IS that connection! You just have to tap into it! It's like a direct line to God himself!

As for recognizing God's voice, the first thing you'll want to do is get a Bible—it's God's word for us, to see who HE is—whether paper-based, a Bible app , or online online. A paper Bible is wonderful because you have to purposely sit down, and block everything out to read it. Read about who He is, and how He loves you. And when you start speaking to God, it doesn't matter how pretty it sounds, or if it sounds silly to you to be talking when there's no one there to hear it. Just start, remembering that God can hear you, and he WANTS to have that relationship with you. Soon you'll start knowing the voice of God when you hear it, and recognize it just like your parents, spouse, friends, and even your kids. Being business partners with God is great! But having God there for EVERY aspect of your life is *amazing*.

Your Direct Sales friend,

Karen

Notes & References

[1] Refer to Matthew 1:5 (ESV)

[2] Day 9: Becky Spieth, The Christian Direct Seller, Success Coaching, March 2013 Conference Call

[3] Day 11: Joshua 23:13, Judges 2:3 Because they didn't follow God's law to destroy everyone, these people would ensnare them later. In 2 Samuel 3:3, David would marry a princess from Geshur. Absolom, born of her, would return there and use it as a place to plot against David

[4] Day 16: Becky Spieth, The Christian Direct Seller, Success Coaching, March 2013

[5] Day 19: Comparison is the thief of Joy, attributed to Theodore Roosevelt

ACKNOWLEDGMENTS

A huge thank you to my family, who gave up free time with their wife and mommy for almost a year as each sentence was lovingly handcrafted, tweaked, and revised. To quote my husband: "What do you mean you're editing AGAIN?" Funny, funny guy.

To my friend Heather Boyll, who never once in twenty-two years let me forget that no matter what else I had going on in life, underneath it all there would always be a writer waiting to tell a story. Thank you for never giving up on me. I love you, dear friend.

To Karen Crossett, who proofread every page and made me fix things that didn't "flow"–You refused to accept a piece until it was perfect. I could not have asked God for a better springboard this year. You thought I was kidding when I told you that you were meant for this project. Thank you for more things than I could begin to list. P.S. Thanks for being my "monkey backpack."

To Keith Crossett, you are awesome. Thanks for sharing YOUR Karen with me this past few months. You rock.

To Susan, thank you for allowing me to write the devotions for our retreat and for recognizing the gifts we all bring to Suzie's Dream Team.

To Team Trinity: You are all simply amazing. I LOVE being your Director!

To God, who gave me a love of books and writing that could never be hidden, no matter how hard I tried. Thank you that there are no chance meetings, and thank you for choosing *me* to receive the whispers of your heart to share with my direct selling sisters. This book is my offering to you, my King.

And to you, New Friend. Thank you for buying this book and recommending it to a friend. May it bless you and your business, and bring you closer to the God who so lovingly created you.

XOXO, Karen

About the Author

Long before she was a wife, mother, and direct sales leader, Karen loved words. Sometimes those words would get her in trouble, like the time in elementary school when she was caught sitting on the kitchen counter reading a book instead of washing dishes. She would still rather read a book than wash dishes, by the way.

Her early works were in children's stories and you can still catch her making up stories for them just about every day. Believing that children today seem to have been robbed of the innocent childhood from yesteryear, she formed a website to return childhood to children... one story at a time. She offers those stories to parents, teachers, and missionaries, so they don't have to worry about making up a story at the end of their crazy, hectic day. You can connect with her on that website at christianbedtimestories.com. One day when she's a gozillionaire, she would love to visit orphanages and homeless shelters with paperback copies of her stories to give to children who need a little glimmer of hope in their life.

Seeing she was not the only one who almost gave up on her life dream, Karen's heart was later pricked for women who felt the same as she once did; that God's plans for them had a deadline for departure and they'd missed the boat. She formed the She Is Free Mission, to encourage women of all ages to realize God's not through with them yet! Her desire is to help them break free of the chains and demands they place on themselves, and evolve into the woman God wants them to be! You can connect with her on her personal blog, sheisfreemission.blogspot.com.

When she's not writing, reading, leading her team, or working with her husband in their travel agency, she is playing outside with the kids and pretending like her house is spotlessly clean. (Hey, it's a tough job but someone's got to do it.) She lives in the south with her husband and twins because there is an unlimited supply of sweet tea, porch swings, and year-round flowers. Every now and then after the snow melts, she'll venture north to her hometown to visit friends and team mates.